Know
WHAT
You
Believe

Know
WHAT
You
Believe

PAUL E. LITTLE

Updated and Expanded by Marie Little

Cook Communications

Victor is an imprint of
Cook Communications Ministries, Colorado Springs, Colorado 80918
Cook Communications, Paris, Ontario, Canada
Kingsway Communications, Eastbourne, England

Editors: Afton Rorvik and Greg Clouse
Study Questions: Afton Rorvik
Cover Design: Bill Gray
Interior Design: RJS Design
Cover Photo: Image Bank

¹ 5 6 7 8 9 10 Printing / Year 03 02 01

Library of Congress Cataloging-in-Publication Data

Little, Paul E.
          Know what you believe/by Paul Little.
                    p.   cm.
          [Updated, new ed.].
          Includes bibliographical references.
          ISBN 1-56476-755-8
                    1. Theology, Doctrinal--Popular works.   I. Title.
BT77.L555   1999   98-43448
230--dc21   CIP

Contents

Preface

It Doesn't Matter What You Think of Play-Doh®, Napoleon, or Richard Nixon. It Does Matter What You Think of Jesus Christ.

Some men write books in an ivory tower, shut off from the world with paper and pen (or computer). The author of this book, my husband, was not one of this kind. Paul wrote his books in the midst of a packed schedule of travel, lectures, and "eyeball-to-eyeball" conversations with university students. He began talking about his faith while still a student at the Wharton School, University of Pennsylvania. When he graduated, he turned from accounting to a full-time career of telling the message of Jesus Christ to the student world. He took his message to schools from coast to coast in the United States and to five continents. It seemed his suitcase was incessantly either being packed or unpacked!

In the course of his relentless schedule, Paul learned to capture his audiences with extraordinary wit. He'd say: "It doesn't matter what you think of Play-Doh®, Napoleon, or Richard Nixon. It *does* matter what you think of Jesus Christ." Or he'd invent graphic illustrations such as: "The Christian experience is not like a man with a fried egg on his ear who claims the egg gives him peace and joy. Rather, the Christian experience is securely bound to the objective, historical fact of the life, death, and resurrection of Jesus Christ."

Whether in a university or in a church, Paul beamed his logic toward the nontheologian, the person in the classroom or the pew. Partial truths and misconceptions about the Christian message hung heavy on Paul's soul until he began to write something on paper. Those writings became *Know What You Believe*. The book highlights the bottom-line truths, the non-negotiables of Christianity. Paul explained these truths to help us understand the magnitude of what God has done to bring us into a relationship with Him through Jesus Christ.

In this new edition, I have inserted some relevant thoughts from Paul's many files and in a few cases placed them in contemporary settings and quotes. It is still entirely Paul's original work. Should readers have critical questions about the Christian faith, Paul's book *Know Why You Believe* aims at answering these. To know *why and what* you believe is a winning combination with divine implications for comprehending the love and grace of God.

After Paul's death in an automobile accident twenty-three years ago, many letters came to me. The following one expresses more eloquently than I could the power of God's message through His Son Jesus Christ.

My husband and I were having problems getting along. I thought it would do him good to read *Know What You Believe*. But when I began reading it myself, I realized I was not a Christian. I knelt down and prayed to the Lord. Now we are both trusting the Lord, and our relationship has been completely healed.

B.C., Chicago, Illinois

Marie Little
Mt. Prospect, Illinois

The Bible

Wh at is the Bible—this Book that has far and away been the bestseller of all history and has been translated into more languages than any other book?

Bible means "book." But what kind of book is the Bible? Some suggest it is a record of man's religious striving toward and encounters with God—an essentially human book. Traditionally, the historic Christian church has seen the Bible as far more than this—namely, as the written Word of God. The first words of the book show that God is the leading character of this divine autobiography: "In the beginning God. . . ." He is the leading character and remains the centerpiece.

The question of the Bible is a crucial one because it holds the key to knowing for certain that God exists. And how can we know about Him, if He *does* exist? Clearly, our finite minds cannot penetrate God's infinity. Job's friend asked him, "Can you fathom the mysteries of God? Can you probe the limits of the Almighty?" (Job 11:7) The answers come through God's "revelation," His taking the initiative and revealing Himself.

In the Bible, His chosen instrument, God unfolds for us His true char-acter. Through everyday human histories He tells us where we came from, what our ultimate destiny is, and the purpose of our lives. He gives practical instructions, heart-thumping encouragements, warnings, and divine wisdom. All from our Creator. Here God's unrivaled power and integrity are also unveiled.

The people God used to record His words were themselves uncom-monly moved by them. They said the Word of God is

- honey in my mouth[a]
- spiritual food for the hungry[b]
- dwelling in me richly[c]
- a lamp for my feet[d]
- a joy and delight to my heart[e]
- renewing my mind[f]
- a fire that burns in my heart[g]

- more precious than gold[h]
- sharper than a two-edged sword[i]
- a great reward[j]
- true and righteous[k]
- penetrating my thoughts and attitudes[l]
- perfect and trustworthy[m]

Unlike these reactions, a student once told me, "When I read the Bible, I fall asleep." Perhaps he overlooked the fact that it was *the God of the universe* who spoke these words. When this gets into the marrow of our bones, the words fly off the pages to us and are nothing short of life-changing.

Today, our need for the Bible, God's Word, is more important than ever. Our world is bombarded with ideas, however well-intentioned, that challenge the time-honored concepts of the God of the Bible. Ideas such as "All roads lead to Rome" and "There is no One Way" come from every corner of the globe. Relativism has taken over, disavowing all possibility of one truth source; postmodernism has arrived, bringing its elastic morality; secularism joins in exalting existential experience.

God Unmasked

By contrast, God, the Creator, has revealed Himself, unmasked Himself, as we would to a friend. He has done this in several ways.

---

[a]Ezek. 3:3; [b]Job 23:12; [c]Col. 3:16; [d]Ps. 119:105; [e]Jer. 15:16; [f]Rom. 12:12; [g]Jer. 20:9; [h]Ps. 19:10; [i]Heb. 4:12; [j]Ps. 19:11; [k]Ps.119:160; [l]Heb. 4:12; [m]Ps. 19:7.

1. *Nature* and the entire creation blare the message of a powerful Designer. Our natural world, down to the most minute atom, the DNA, RNA, and the innumerable galaxies shout the Designer's intelligence. "For since the creation of the world God's invisible qualities—his eternal power and divine nature—have been clearly seen, being understood from what has been made" (Rom. 1:20). "The heavens declare the glory of God. . . . There is no speech or language where their voice is not heard" (Ps. 19:1, 3).

2. Through *history* God has revealed Himself, particularly in His dealings with Israel and the nations surrounding her. Such Old Testament expressions as "Then Manasseh knew that the Lord is God" (2 Chron. 33:13) reflect recognition of God because of His activity in the affairs of individuals and nations.

Isaiah 63:8-9 pictures God's *persistent reaching out to Israel:* "'Surely they are my people, sons who will not be false to me'; and so he became their Savior. In all their distress he too was distressed, and the angel of his presence saved them. In his love and mercy he redeemed them; he lifted them up and carried them all the days of old."

3. The *words of the prophets* were also instruments of God's revelation as they *interpreted* the events and God's will. "The word of the Lord came to me" and "This is what the Lord says . . ." are recurring phrases throughout the Old Testament (Ezek. 6:1, 7:1, 12:1; Zech. 8:1; Ex. 4:22; 1 Sam. 2:27), called propositional revelation.

God's Special Revelation

Jesus Christ was God's fullest and clearest revelation. He was God incarnate. "The image of the invisible God," "The Word became flesh," and "We beheld His glory" are but a few descriptions of Jesus Christ. The writers in Hebrews and Acts explained it this way: "In the past God spoke to our forefathers through the prophets at many times and in various ways, but in these last days he has spoken to us by his Son" (Heb 1:1-2). "All the prophets testify about him [Jesus] that everyone who believes in him receives forgiveness of sins through his name" (Acts 10:43).

THE BIBLE'S TWO SECTIONS		
	Old Testament	**New Testament**
Number of Books	39	27
Major Groups	Law, Historical Books, Poetry, Wisdom, Prophets	Gospels, Acts, Epistles, Revelation
Years to Write	1,100 years	100 years

Written Record Needed

But what about people who were not present and so did not see God's involvement in history or the events surrounding Christ's incarnation, life, death, and resurrection? To reach *all* generations, obviously, a written record was needed, one that would touch all people everywhere. And the Bible was God's chosen vehicle.

The Bible consists of two sections, the Old Testament and the New Testament. (See the chart for details.) The Old Testament was written over 1,100 years; the New Testament was written within the span of a century.

Testament means "covenant," an alliance between two partners, an "agreement," a "promise." The Old Testament covenant was brought to fulfillment in the New Testament. Through Israel, the entire world would learn of God's covenant to send a redeemer.

God's covenant was first specifically enunciated to Abraham (then Abram). It covered three aspects: a *land* for Israel, a *nation* (numbered more than the stars in the heaven) and *blessing to all the people of the earth* (the Redeemer to bring God's forgiveness). See Genesis 12:1-3 and 15:4-7.[1]

Languages

The Old Testament was written in Hebrew. A gradual infiltration of the Greek language came with the expansion of the Greek empire under Alexander the Great from Greece to Persia in 331 B.C., including Palestine. Through several centuries, Greek culture dominated until the Romans conquered the land under Pompey in 66 B.C.

Jesus was born into a Hebrew culture in which the spoken language was a "common" form of Hebrew called Aramaic and a "common" form of Greek called Koine. Hence the New Testament was written by Jewish people, largely in common Greek.

A Greek translation of the Hebrew Old Testament, called the Septuagint (meaning seventy), was made by a group of seventy-two Jewish scholars about 250 B.C. for the Israelites. It was necessary because of the impact of Hellenism on Judaism.[2] The books were arranged according to similarity of subject matter, and this is the order of our Protestant Bible today.

With the spread of Christianity to Rome, the Latin Vulgate version was translated in roughly A.D. 400. It became the authorized version of the Catholic Church. Twelve books, called the Apocrypha (meaning hidden), were included in this version. They were never included in the Hebrew Old Testament or in the Protestant editions today. (New Testament writers quoted from every other book of the Old Testament except the Apocrypha.)

There were no chapter and verse divisions until around the year A.D. 1214, when the books were divided into chapters. Over 300 years later, verses were given numbers.

Inspired!

How was a book of history covering over 2,000 years written? And how could it have a single theme? Two clear statements from the New Testament answer this question: "Understand that no prophecy of Scripture came about by the prophet's own interpretation. For prophecy never had its origin in the will of man, but men spoke from God as they were carried along by the Holy Spirit" (2 Peter 1:20-21). "All Scripture is God-breathed and is useful for teaching, rebuking, correcting and training in righteousness" (2 Tim. 3:16).

The Bible originated in the mind of God, not in the mind of man. It was given to man by *inspiration*. The Bible is not inspired as we say the writings of Shakespeare were inspired or the music of Bach was inspired. The biblical sense of inspiration means: *God so superintended the writers of Scripture that they wrote what He wanted them to write, disclosing the exact truth He wanted conveyed.*

The word *inspired* literally means "outbreathed" (from the mouth of God). Timothy is unambiguous; the words did not come from the writers themselves! Inspiration applies to the end result—the Scripture itself—a faulty script would be useless.

Every Word Inspired

Assent to the fact of the inspiration of the Bible can be a superficial nod of the head or a heartfelt awe over God's intentional reaching out to each of us. Three terms help us understand the truth of inspiration.

1. *"Plenary inspiration"* means *all* of Scripture is inspired—not merely some parts. (*Plenary* means full.) Implicit in God's act of "plenary inspiration" is His disclosure of exactly what we need to know about Him, no more, no less. He communicated His basic plans and promises for all of His creation.

2. *"Verbal inspiration"* indicates that inspiration extends to the *words* of the Bible themselves, not only to the ideas. God did not dictate the Scripture mechanically, but guided and superintended the writers within the framework of their own personalities and backgrounds. This guidance would of necessity include their choice of words, since thoughts are composed of words, much as a theme of music consists of individual notes. Altering the notes alters the song.

3. *"Plenary, verbal inspiration"* stresses the authenticity and reliability of the very words that were written, without depriving the writers of their individuality. A Christian who has such a high view of inspiration exam-

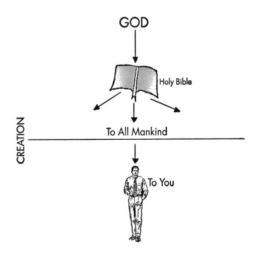

ines prayerfully the meaning of each word and remains sincerely interested in using modern tools of textual study to understand the original
meaning.

God Guarded Each Copy

The inspiration of the Scripture applies only to the text *as originally produced by the writers*. Those *original* writings were without error.

Through the centuries (before typewriters or computers), copyists did
meticulous work. These copyists worked with such precision and reverence that they wiped their pens clean each time before writing the name
of God. We now have thousands of miraculously preserved copies, differing from each other in only minute ways. One scholar likened the differences to the English spellings of *honor* and *honour*, both considered cor-
rect.

God sovereignly *guarded* and protected the copies (those we have
now).

The Writers Not Automatons

God chose writers whose hearts were receptive to Him, yet each one was
uniquely different. They were not human typewriters, used by God. He
wants no automatons.

First of all, the full personalities of the writers entered into their writings. Secondly, the individual writing styles of the authors are evident,
some obviously reflecting more education than others. The writers of the
Psalms were diverse, some poets, some singers, etc. Though their human
capacities came into play, all of these writers were superintended and
borne along in a unique way by the Holy Spirit as they each wrote from
a different perspective.

However the words came to be recorded, *all* Scripture is viewed by the
writers themselves as words from God, not from their own minds. The
Apostle Paul speaks of Scripture as "the very words of God" (Rom. 3:2).

Jesus Himself quoted the Old Testament as the counsel of God given
through the writers. The early believers prayed in Acts, "Sovereign Lord
. . . You spoke by the Holy Spirit through the mouth of your servant, our
father David," then they quoted Psalm 2:1-2 (Acts 4:24-25).

Benjamin Warfield pointed out that such instances of equating
Scriptures *as if they were God* resulted from the writer's habitual identifi-

cation of Scripture with God. It became natural to use the terms "Scripture says" and "God says" synonymously.[3]

Some Words Are from Evil People

To say *all* Scripture is inspired does not mean all the attitudes and ideas are God's truth. Some are the words of evil and foolish people, even of Satan himself. Such parts are recorded as accurate information, true pictures of the people's words and the circumstances.

In the Book of Job we are told the words of Jehovah, the words of Satan, the speeches of Job's three friends, and the words of Job himself. Not all are equally God's truth and authoritative, but inspiration guarantees that what each speaker said was accurately recorded. A good rule for any passage is to check the participants and their belief systems.

A few scholars have implied that the Bible "contains" the Word of God rather than "is" the Word of God in its entirety. If this were true, how would we know which parts are trustworthy and which are not? Often salvation and history are inextricably intertwined. For example, if the Cross and the Resurrection were not historical events, of what value are they in salvation? Personal subjective judgment is a shaky foundation on which to base our faith.

Which Books Are Inspired?

The Bible, as we know it today, is called the "canon" of Scripture, that is those books recognized as inspired. In our Lord's time, the Old Testament was viewed as a completed collection. He and the apostles referred to this

HOW WRITERS WERE INSPIRED		
	Method	**Events**
1	God described directly to the writer	The creation of the universe and human race (Gen. 1–2)
2	Writers actually witnessed	The Resurrection and Jesus' miracles (John 20:3-9)
3	Copied from other texts handed down from eyewitnesses	The creation of Luke's gospel (Luke 1:1-4)
4	God spoke directly to the prophets	"This is what the Lord . . . says" (Jer. 30:1-2)

collection as "the Scripture." Most of the books of the Old Testament are quoted in the New and always as authoritative. According to careful calculation, approximately 32 percent—nearly one-third—of the New Testament is composed of Old Testament quotations and allusions.[4]

The canon of the New Testament, as we know it today, became fixed when Athanasius (A.D. 297–373), considered the father of orthodoxy, listed the books of the New Testament in his thirty-ninth Paschal Letter (A.D. 367). Our canon today was also confirmed at a church council held in Carthage in A.D. 397. Three criteria were used in recognizing canonicity:

- Was a book apostolic in origin?
- Was the book used and recognized by the churches?
- Did the book teach sound doctrine?[5]

Based on answers to these three questions, the orthodox Protestant church today does not receive as canonical the twelve books of the Apocrypha. Also, the Jews never recognized these books as part of their Old Testament.

The Primary Source of Religious Belief

Can we really trust the Bible as our primary source of religious belief? Generally, scholars have discussed four sources for religious belief.

> # The Bible is our sole truth source.

1. The first possible source for our beliefs is *tradition*, the authority of a particular church. This is the view of Roman Catholics and other groups.

2. The second source is *human reason*, a view often adopted by well-read thinkers. Human reason could include other religions or philosophies as well as unfounded ideas such as those of Joseph Smith finding buried tablets and palm readers or psychics telling the future. Such ideas are missing a rational truth source.

3. A third recently popularized source of belief is an *existential encounter* or an emotional experience of any variety. These can be mistaken as God's revelation.

4. The fourth source of belief is *the Bible itself,* which Christians have recognized as supported and verified by rational investigation and the historicity of Jesus Christ Himself. To take this position does not deny tradition or human reason, but it does demand that all beliefs be submitted to the message of Scripture. Based on repeatedly accredited evidence of modern archaeology, we can trust the Bible with confidence. God's truth remains our reality.

Tips on Interpreting a Biblical Passage

Biblical understanding and interpretation can be oversimplified as either "literal" or "figurative." As in reading anything, including the daily newspaper, some parts of the Bible are to be taken literally and other parts figuratively.

> **"I use Scripture as a lighter to kindle the fire in my heart."**
> *Martin Luther*

The Bible uses literary forms such as poetry, allegory, narrative, and parable. Though some passages are more perplexing than others, usually common sense helps understanding. The statement "Two people were killed in an accident on Main Street" is obviously literal. "He shot home from third in the last half of the ninth with the winning run under his arm, and the crowd went mad" contains readily recognized figurative language. A player does not "shoot" home or carry runs under his arm. And the fans in the bleachers, though they may get excited, do not become insane.

• *Figures of speech* can be recognized by considering the intent of the author. Look through his eyes for his meaning. The Bible is replete with metaphors such as, "I am the door" and "I am the vine, you are the branches." Obviously, these sentences are not talking about a literal door or wood or tree branches.

• The *context* of a chapter or book is an excellent starting point for understanding a biblical passage. Statements lifted out of their context can become entirely distorted, even developing into unbiblical doctrines. A skeptic once triumphantly asserted, "The Bible says, 'There is no God.'" He was considerably deflated when reminded of the context: "The fool says in his heart, 'There is no God' " (Ps. 14:1).

• Who is the *writer* or *speaker*; who is addressed? What is the relationship between the two?

• *What is the primary teaching of the passage?*

• Is there *application* for us? The importance of this cannot be overemphasized. This is applying God's Word to our own lives, personalizing biblical truth and living by it. Application can be *universal*, applied to all people, everywhere; or application can be *limited*, applied to specific situations, present or future.

• *Meditate* on any truth about God, Jesus, or the Holy Spirit. "Through the sacred pages, I see You, Lord." Munch on these truths, letting them affect your relationship with God. Write these truths in your own words. Pray to Him about these truths.

• The *Scripture is its own best commentary*. Often a verse or a passage becomes clear when studied in the light of other biblical statements on the same subject. Look up a key word in a concordance. Using a good Bible dictionary or a general dictionary to investigate the full meaning of the words of Scripture will reveal surprising riches. Try it! And consult several translations.

Though the Bible has many human writers, remind yourself constantly that in the final analysis there was only one Author—God Himself.

Does the Sun Rise?

Perhaps the most common challenge to the Bible today is this: do scientific facts and statements in the Bible conflict? How should we respond?

• Scientists, and all of us, speak in what is called *phenomenological* language—that is, we describe things *as they appear to be* rather than in precise scientific terms. This is common in the Bible. To say the sun rises in the east is a phenomenological statement. Technically, we know the sun does not really "rise," but even the *Naval Almanac* uses the term *sunrise*. We would not charge the almanac with error. The Bible has been easily understood in all cultures throughout history because it describes things in a phenomenological way. *The Bible does not claim to be a science textbook*, but where it touches scientific matters, *it does not give misinformation*.

• When Bible information is *incomplete*, it is not necessarily *incorrect*. Science is always building on previous knowledge, sometimes scraps of knowledge. Advancement on incomplete theories does not mean the theories were incorrect.

• Guard against making the Bible say things that, on closer examination, it really *doesn't say*.

• Carefully investigate whether the supposed conflict is between biblical teaching and scientific facts or between *interpretation* of Scripture and *interpretation* of scientific facts. At times an interpretation at variance with biblical truth is more philosophic than scientific.

• Our presuppositions inevitably color our conclusions, thus the Christian, the scientist, and the atheist all consider spiritual truth with prior presuppositions. For example, an atheist can *a priori* eliminate the possibility of miracles while a Christian presupposes there is a mighty God who can and would do miracles. Christians base their presuppositions on God's *general revelation*, His *written revelation*, and His *special revelation*, Jesus Christ.

• Be careful not to *"freeze" a point of conflict* between science and God's revelation, assuming the Bible to be wrong. The Bible has not changed in 2,000 years, but science admittedly is a moving train. To have reconciled the Bible to scientific views current 100 years ago would have made Scripture obsolete today! Far better to *admit* an apparent conflict and await the development of additional evidence.

It is interesting to note that modern science was born and developed largely by earnest Christians. Believing in a personal God as Creator, they were convinced that the universe was orderly and uniform in its natural laws and therefore capable of meaningful investigation. The truth of biblical revelation and the truth of science will ultimately agree. All truth is from God.

Dating Problems Explained

In careful reading it may appear the Bible has some "internal" contradictions in parallel accounts of the same event. Some apparent numerical differences may be due to mistakes in copying over many years. Recent archaeological discoveries, however, show the ancients' system of dating explains some numerical problems. If, for example, *one king ended his rule and another began ruling in a given calendar year,* both were given credit for ruling the entire year. Round numbers like our police estimates are often used—not precise, but not incorrect.

Some explanations for seeming biblical discrepancies may not be currently satisfactory. Yet, it would be unscientific, in light of modern archaeological discoveries, to assume the Bible is wrong until proven right, rather than the reverse.

An ever increasing number of excavations from Egypt to Babylonia have told us more about the life and history of Bible lands. Thousands of records etched in stone tablets dating back to 3,000 years before Christ have been quarried and subsequently translated. Alan R. Millard, senior lecturer at the University of Liverpool, states: "All of these discoveries have increased our knowledge of the world in which the Bible was written, so they enable its distinctive message to stand out more boldly. Rightly interpreted, the Bible and archaeology can only enrich each other."[6]

To believe in divine, biblical inspiration is not to deny there are problems reconciling some statements of Scripture with the historical data we possess. But the evidence of modern archeaology has, with very few exceptions, confirmed the Bible record, so it would not seem unreasonable to postpone judgment on the questions still in doubt.

We do not "prove" the Bible by archaeology. The Holy Spirit confirms in our hearts the conviction "the Bible is the Word of God."

Holy Spirit Illumination Is Essential

Scripture becomes meaningful to individuals when their hearts are open and illumined by the Holy Spirit. Jesus asked Peter the climactic question, "Who do you say I am?" and Peter's immediate response was, "You are the Christ, the Son of the living God." Jesus then said, "Blessed are you, Simon son of Jonah, for this was not revealed to you by man, but by *my Father* in heaven" (Matt. 16:15-17, italics added).

Again, when Jesus met two disciples on the road to Emmaus following His resurrection, He "explained to them what was written in all the Scriptures concerning himself." As He sat with them, "their eyes were opened and they recognized him" (Luke 24:27, 31). "Then He opened their minds so they could understand the Scriptures" (24:45). He also explicitly told His disciples, "When he, the Spirit of truth, comes, he will guide you into all truth" (John 16:13). God reveals by the Spirit what He has prepared for those who love Him (1 Cor. 2:9-10).

The Bible does not *become* the Word of God; it *is* already the Word of God. A television set, sitting in the corner but not turned on, is still a television set. I won't get any images or sound until I turn it on, but it *is* a television set, whether turned on or not. It doesn't *become* a television set when turned on. What the Holy Spirit illumines is the Word of God, not something less. It doesn't *become* something it wasn't before.

Furthermore, the Scripture *is* the Word of God, whether or not anybody even responds to it. We have the choice. We can open our minds and hearts to the Holy Spirit, thus allowing the Scripture to become *personal* to our lives.

"Necessary Food"

"Never study the Bible for purely academic purposes" was the admonition of scholar Martyn Lloyd-Jones. Beyond its sacred pages, we connect personally to God. Academic understanding does help illumine our thoughts, but then we must turn to speak to the Author, react to His words, probe His will for our lives.

One well-known performer said: "Nothing outside yourself can make you feel whole. Not fame, not sex, not drugs, not money. None of these work. Nothing can fill you up. And believe me, because I've tried them all."[7]

By contrast, the Old Testament's Job, a man in horrendous loss and suffering, gives us a glimpse of how to approach God's Word. In the midst of his suffering, he said in his talk with God: "I have treasured the words of [your] mouth more than my necessary food" (Job 23:12, NKJV). Just as food gets to the muscles and bloodstream, the words from God can make you feel whole, satisfied, loved, connected—deep inside!

Our faith is rooted in the Bible, but we do not worship it, we trust it. Every new idea and even our emotional experiences are to be tested by its teaching. Are my opinions, my world views, and my actions congruent with God's revelation?

By all means, anticipate joy and exhilaration as you respond to God's words. Blaise Pascal, the renowned French scientist, sought diligently to know God, and the fruit of his search is expressed in very moving lines. Some were written on paper and sewn inside his coat and discovered after he died! One of them was:

O righteous Father, the world hath not known Thee,
But I have known Thee. Joy. Joy. Joy. Tears of joy.[8]

Your Word, O Lord, is eternal; it stands firm in the heavens. (Ps. 119:89)

GOD

W hat we believe about God," said the late A.W. Tozer, "is the most important thing about us." Our belief or lack of it inevitably translates itself into our actions, our attitudes, and our view of the world.

It is interesting to construct the kind of God the Old Testament character Joseph believed in based on his reactions to his traitorous brothers, followed by his unjust imprisonment by an official. In the end, he looked back at his brothers and concluded: "Am I in the place of God? You intended to harm me, but God intended it for good" (Gen. 50:19-20).

Then, consider Moses, who left the king's palace for God's people and the desert. He "persevered because he saw him who is invisible" (Heb. 11:27). Significantly, Hebrews 11 lists many faithful followers, describing them by what they *did* rather than what they *said* or *professed*.

The word *God* itself is one of the most widely used terms in our language; yet it is nebulous and undefined in most minds. Typically, we hear God is

"a pure mathematical mind" (Einstein's early statement),

"a shadowy superhuman cloud or force,"
"a ball of fire ready to consume us,"
"sparks of life to which we will be reunited,"
"a sentimental grandfather in the sky," or
"a fearful celestial policeman."

Our broadly secular world has made it easy for us to use the word *God* and resist trying to define Him, often times only for the sake of avoiding division. Think for a moment. If God *is*, His existence and what He is like do not really depend on what anyone thinks about Him. To conceive of God as a stone idol or a mystical idea does not *make* Him either. These could not communicate to us let alone reveal themselves.

If we are interested in *reality*, we will want to know what God is *really* like. When we explore God through His general and special revelation, we build our own personal foundation and information bank.

> **The most frequently asked question is not whether God exists, but whether God is good.**

Then, based on His communication with us, we can confidently judge as true or false the ideas and images of God that exist today. Our personal concept of God—when we pray, for instance—is *worthless* unless it is coherent and coincides with His self-revelation.

God's "Natural" Attributes

The terms that describe the nature of God are known as His attributes. They are classified as "natural" attributes and "moral" attributes. Let's think first about God's "natural" attributes, all revealed by His self-disclosure in Scripture.

• God is *transcendent, excels above all,* and is separate from His creation, above and beyond it. He is self-existing and not only has life in Himself but is also the source of all life. Words like *supreme* and *incomparable* come to mind. He is not a slave to natural law. He authored it but is independent of it and above it. He can override it at will—though normally He does not interfere with it. He is exalted and eternal, the world's Creator, Sovereign, and Judge.

The prophet spoke of God's *transcendence* when he wrote of "the high and lofty One . . . who lives forever, whose name is holy [set apart]" (Isa. 57:15). God is not so totally transcendent that He set the universe in motion and then left it, like winding a clock and letting it wind down. (This is generally what deists believe.)

• God is *immanent, near,* as well as transcendent. By this we mean that His presence and power pervade His entire creation. He does not stand apart from the world, a mere spectator of the things He has made. As Isaiah explains, God is "with him who is contrite and lowly in spirit, to revive the spirit of the lowly and to revive the heart of the contrite" (Isa. 57:15).

He is not so immanent, however, that He is indistinguishable from the universe. Pantheism holds that God is all and that all is God. But that means you and I would be part of God, which ultimately means that God sins when we sin. One such believer in pantheism told me as proof, "If I touch this table, it presses back." If all is God, and everything else is illusion, as some hold, then what could exist to have the illusion? Does God have illusions? Undoubtedly, one can marvel at the handiwork of God in nature yet not embrace pantheism.

• God is *omnipotent, all-powerful.* The Bible tells us the universe God has made speaks of His eternal power *(omnipotence)* and deity (Rom. 1:19-20). The Rocky Mountains, Niagara Falls, the starry hosts of heaven, the oceans' vastness—all remind us that God made them and is sovereign over them.

The prophet observed, "Ah, Sovereign Lord, you have made the heavens and the earth by your great power and outstretched arm. Nothing is too hard for you" (Jer. 32:17). The angel Gabriel assured Mary, after informing her of her privilege of bearing the Son of God as a virgin, "Nothing is impossible with God" (Luke 1:37).

The omnipotence of God has intrinsic limitations, self-imposed, as it were. He is intentionally limited by His moral character. For example, though "nothing is impossible with God," Hebrews 6:18 tells us, "it is impossible for God to lie." His omnipotence applies to inherent possibilities, not inherent impossibilities. Someone once asked, "Is it possible for God to make anything too heavy for Himself to lift? If not, how can we say He is omnipotent?" C.S. Lewis would say, "Nonsense is still nonsense," whether we are talking about something else or about God.[1]

• God is *omnipresent, in all places, all the time.* He is fully present everywhere. He is not like a substance spread out in a thin layer all over the earth. *All* of Him is within each one of us—His power, knowledge, and all His other characteristics. As you read these words and as you leave your home, go to work, etc., He is there with you. He is in Chicago, in Calcutta, in Cairo, and in Caracas, at one and the same time.

• God is *omniscient, knows everything.* This includes our actions and our thoughts. David wrote, "You know when I sit and when I rise; you perceive my thoughts from afar" (Ps. 139:2). The Apostle John watched Jesus' actions and wrote, "He did not need man's testimony about man, for He knew what was in a man" (John 2:25). Isaiah quoted God directly saying, "I am God, and there is no other; I am God, and there is none like me. I make known the end from the beginning" (Isa. 46:9-10). Nothing surprises God.

• God is *eternal, timeless.* He never had a beginning and will never have an end. As observed earlier, He is the "One . . . who lives forever" (Isa. 57:15). "The eternal God is your refuge" (Deut. 33:27). To the common question "Who created God?" the answer is "No one and nothing." There was never a time when He did not exist. God's existence preceded time as we know it, and He created time.[2]

• God is *infinite, unlimited.* He is not limited by or confined to the universe He created. He is independent of finite (measurable) things and beings, even time and space. God has, however, chosen to put limitations on Himself on some occasions. For instance, He appeared to Old Testament believers in the form of an angel or a man. (See Gen. 18:1.) He also became incarnate in the person of Jesus Christ. In His incarnation, He imposed voluntary limits on Himself in order to bless His creatures and accomplish His purposes, not because He *had* to.[3]

Our minds do not adequately conceive of an *infinite* quantity of anything—space, power, potatoes. Such concepts baffle and frustrate us. We *can*, however, imagine a being—God—who has no limitations in His character attributes. In His holiness, for instance, He has no limitations and no defects. The same may be said for each of His other qualities. His power (omnipotence) is at work and in control of everything, anywhere, that exists.[4]

• God is *unchangeable, does not vary*. He "does not change like shifting shadows," as James expressed it (1:17). Unlike human beings, God is not volatile or capricious. His love is steadfast and constant and is not subject to the ebb and flow of human love. His attitude toward sin is a fixed attitude, not like our fits of temper when something displeases us. He is unchangeably against injustice, cruelty, or deceit.

We cannot easily grasp the idea of such an unchanging God. Consider the man who walks east into a strong east wind and then turns around and walks west. He mistakenly says, "The wind was on my face, but now it is on my back." There has actually been no change in the wind. It was his direction that changed, and this change brought him into a new relationship with the wind. God never changes. When He *seems* to be different, it might be because *we* have changed and in so doing have come into a different relationship with Him.

The Bible speaks of God as "changing His mind," and "having compassion" in the story of Jonah. These terms describe what *seems* to us as God's change. God saw the intransigent evil of the ancient city of Nineveh and threatened to destroy it. To give the people warning, He sent Jonah to talk to them. They heard Jonah preach and turned to God for forgiveness. God saw how they repented, and "He had compassion and did not bring upon them the destruction He had threatened" (Jonah 3:10). God Himself had not changed, the people repented.

God Is Personal

We have saved for last the fact about God that, among His "natural" attributes, is of greatest importance.

• God is *personal; He is a person*. He is all-wise, infinite, eternal, and changeless. We are not to think of Him as an impersonal force behind

Invisible does not mean nonexistent!

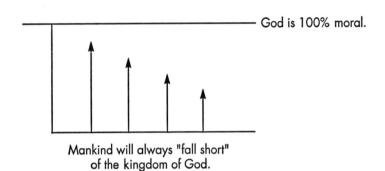

Mankind will always "fall short"
of the kingdom of God.

the universe. God is *spirit* yet has all the elements of personality—intellect, feelings, and will. He acts according to His own purpose and will.

We know this of God because He created man in His own image and after His own likeness (Gen. 1:26). Since *we* are persons, God cannot possibly be something less than a person. What is created cannot be of a higher order than its Creator. Each of the other "natural" attributes is inseparable from His personhood.

Because God is personal, we know that His sovereign will is not akin to the blind fate ("kismet") of Islam's Allah. It is rather the loving purpose of a Heavenly Father to whom His children are precious. And because God is a Person and we are persons, communication between Him and us is possible.

Although God is a spirit, without a physical body, He is nonetheless real. Jesus declared, "God is spirit, and his worshipers must worship in spirit and in truth" (John 4:24). Our spirits can communicate with His spirit, this One who has disclosed Himself as all-powerful, all-wise, infinite, eternal, and changeless.

God's "Moral" Attributes

God's "moral" attributes have inspired poets, the psalmist, and vocalists. To know God exists is only the beginning; to understand His moral nature is of supreme importance. Suppose we believe that this all-powerful God exists, but we think of Him as being like Adolf Hitler. What a horrible prospect to contemplate eternity with such a being. What a heinous existence we would have!

• *Holiness* is *the sum total of the perfection of God,* perhaps the most comprehensive of all of God's attributes. It is a term for the moral excellence of God and His freedom from all *limitations* to His moral perfection: "Your eyes are too pure to look on evil" (Hab. 1:13).[5] In this exalted sense, only God is holy. He is therefore the standard of ethical purity by which His creatures are measured.

Since holiness embraces every distinctive attribute of the Godhead, it may be defined as the outshining of all that God is. As the sun's rays, combining all the colors of the spectrum, come together in the shining of the sun and blending into light, so in God's self-manifestation all the attributes of God come together and blend into holiness. Holiness has, for that reason, been called "the attribute of attributes"—that which lends unity to all the attributes of God.[6]

Moses, out of the fullness of his heart cried, "O Lord, who is like you—majestic in holiness?" (Ex. 15:11) The same Hebrew word is translated "good" in Genesis when God assessed His creative acts. All He does is good, in every act He is free from all imperfection. He cannot even be tempted with evil. We can clearly see God's absolute perfection and His abhorrence of evil through His persistent reaching out to rescue His people and through them rescuing all who will come to Him.

> Can God hear a hundred million prayers at one time? "God has infinite attention to spare for each one of us. He does not deal with us in the mass. You are as much alone with him as if you were the only being he had ever created."
> *C.S. Lewis*

• God is *loving*. His love is *divine, a perfect love*. God's love is displayed in all His works from the beginning of the Old Testament to the end of the New Testament. We see God's love in the creation of the world all the way to the climax of His Son dying on the cross. His love takes concrete action. His acts of creating the world and the human race were born of love. "I led them with cords of human kindness, with ties of love" (Hos. 11:4). "I have loved you with an everlasting love; I have drawn you with loving-kindness" (Jer. 31:3). "This is love: not that we loved God, but that he loved us and sent his Son as an atoning sacrifice for our sin" (1 John 4:10). "For God so loved the world that He gave. . ." (John 3:16).

God is love was ultimately expressed and personified in Jesus' three-year ministry. His countless acts of compassion for the sick, His acceptance of the sinner, His grief-stricken attitude toward human disobedience showed love-in-action. He reached out to become a friend of tax collectors and outcasts, He held little children in His arms. (See Mark 1:41; Luke 15:1; Matt. 23:37; Luke 7:34; Mark 10:16).

Love and Holiness

His love and mercy are not opposed to, or exercised at the expense of His righteousness and holiness. The Apostle John stated simply, "God is love" (1 John 4:8, 16). From beginning to end of His revelation in the Scriptures, God is seen reaching out, undergirding with His everlasting arms (Deut. 33:27). The promise of a Redeemer, the covenant with Israel, and the final giving of eternal life through the cross were all motivated by His love and mercy.

Some people wrongly suggest that the God of the Old Testament is a God of wrath and anger, while the New Testament portrays God in Christ as love and gentleness. These people sometimes imply that these are two different Gods. This, of course, is completely false. The God of the Old Testament, who repeatedly had mercy on the Israelites and saved them from their own perversions, is the same Lord Jesus who wept over Jerusalem because her people killed the prophets and would not turn to the Lord (Matt. 23:37). The Jesus who spoke frequently of hell and eternal judgment is the same God who moved in judgment on Jerusalem in 586 B.C. and on the pagan King Belshazzar of Babylon (Dan. 5:30). Love and justice are knit together.

Our Triune God

At the heart of the Christian view of God is the concept of the *Trinity*. Rather than being "excess baggage," as the late Episcopal bishop James A. Pike called it, this truth is central to an understanding of biblical revelation and the Christian gospel. The word *Trinity* does not occur any-where in the Bible, but the fact is inescapable and does not mean the idea is a later development or a product of philosophic speculation.

The Trinity is a difficult concept, not fully susceptible to human explanation because it involves categories our finite mental powers can-not easily grasp. Anyone who has ever tried to explain the Trinity to an unbeliever will agree that it could hardly be a human invention. It is a teaching that God Himself has revealed to us: *God is one being, but He exists in three persons.*

"God is *one* in His essential being, but the 'divine essence' exists in three modes or forms, each constituting a Person, yet in such a way that the divine essence is wholly in each Person."[7]

The Old Testament begins using the Hebrew word *Elohim* for God, the plural form of the general name *"el,"* meaning God. He is the Beginner and Creator, the Maker and Sustainer. "God, as Creator, thought up the Universe, expressed His thought in a Word, and made His Spirit its ani-mating principle."[8]

The following immortal words were read by Lunar Module Pilot William Anders in Apollo 8 as the spacecraft circled the moon: "In the beginning God created the heaven and the earth. And the earth was without form, and void; and darkness was upon the face of the deep. And the Spirit of God moved upon the face of the waters. And God said, Let there be light: and there was light" (Gen. 1:1-3, KJV).

John explicitly identifies Jesus Christ, the Son, "the Word," with the same three words: "In the beginning." "In the beginning was the Word, and the Word was with God, and the Word was God. He was with God in the beginning. Through him all things were made. . . . The Word became flesh and lived for a while among us. We have seen his glory, the glory of the one and only Son, who came from the Father, full of grace and truth" (John 1:1-3, 14).

The Bible's emphasis throughout, however, is on the fact that God is *one*. "Hear, O Israel: The Lord our God, the Lord is one" (Deut. 6:4). This truth was in sharp contrast to the rampant polytheism that sur-rounded the nation of Israel in Bible times. We must not allow the scrip-tural truth of the Trinity to deprive us of the equally important teaching that there is only *one* God. The Father, Son, and Holy Spirit are *One*.

In the New Testament the distinctness of the persons of the Godhead is made clearer. Our Lord taught the disciples to baptize in *the name* (sin-gular) of the Father and of the Son and of the Holy Spirit (Matt. 28:19), underlining their *Oneness*.

John the Baptist spoke of the coming baptism of the (Holy) Spirit, of which his own water baptism was a symbol. When John baptized Him, Jesus saw "heaven being torn open and the Spirit descending upon him like a dove. And a voice came from heaven: "You are my Son, whom I love; with you I am well pleased" (Mark 1:10-11). This was a clear manifestation of the Trinity, involving *all three persons* of the Godhead.

Earlier, at the birth of Jesus, all three Persons of the Godhead are also mentioned. The angel told Mary that her child would be the *Son of God* conceived by the *Holy Spirit* (Luke 1:35). Jesus explicitly spoke of the Father and the Spirit as being distinct persons from Himself (John 14—16).

Salvation itself portrays the work of the Triune God. The Father sent the Son to accomplish the work of redemption. The Son sent the Spirit to bring conviction and to apply to people's hearts what Christ had accomplished.

The apostolic benediction "The grace of the Lord Jesus Christ, and the love of God, and the fellowship of the Holy Spirit be with you all" (2 Cor. 13:14) is another instance of apostolic teaching on the Trinity. Paul wrote of "God our Father" (Rom. 1:7) and spoke of Christ as the "Son he loves . . . the image of the invisible God" (Col. 1:13, 15) and as "God our Savior" (Titus 3:4). Each person of the Trinity is fully God. Peter told Ananias that in lying to the Holy Spirit, he had "not lied to men but to God" (Acts 5:3-4). The deity of the Holy Spirit is clear.

A Semantic Problem

Part of the problem of understanding the Trinity is the inadequacy of human words to express divine reality. For instance, we speak of the "persons" in the Godhead. We use this term because it describes a being who has intellect, emotion, and will. We can understand this. But we must be careful in applying such terms to God.

"Three persons" is the usual expression, but it is an imperfect term, denoting separate moral or rational individuals. There are not three individuals but *three personal self distinctions* within *one* divine essence.

"Person" used in human terms implies *independence*, not *oneness* of will, actions, and feelings as is true of the Trinity. The Divine Trinity is One self-conscious, self-directing being, yet no part ever acts *independently*, or in *opposition* to the others. God is a unity, His life is not split into three. He is One in essence, in personality, and will.[9]

It is important to understand the relationships of the persons of the Trinity. The Son and the Spirit are said to be "subordinate" to the Father, but this does not mean they are inferior. Their subordination has been called a matter of relationship, but not of nature.

Subordinate Not Inferior

- "The Father, the fount of Deity, *originates*.
- The Son, eternally begotten of the Father, *reveals*.
- The Spirit, eternally proceeding from the Father and the Son, *executes*.

Creation is:
- From the Father
- Through the Son
- By the Holy Spirit."[10]

The Spirit of God is said to proceed from the Son as well as from the Father. The Father is the One by whom the Son is begotten and from whom the Spirit proceeds.

Two Major Heresies about the Trinity

Historically, there have been two major heretical distortions of the Trinity, which are still embraced by some.

One distortion attempted to get away from any implication that there are three separate and distinct persons in the Godhead. Those who held this view claimed that Father, Son, and Holy Spirit are merely *different manifestations* of the one God. He assumes these manifestations temporarily to achieve His purposes. At times God appears as Father, at times as Son, and at times as the Holy Spirit. A man named Sabellius originated this view in the third century A.D.

The second heretical point of view so strongly stressed the persons of the Trinity that the Godhead ended up being *divided*. Those who held this view defined the Son and the Holy Spirit as being lesser, subordinate beings whom the Father willed into existence for the purpose of acting as His agents in His dealings with the world and men. Arius was the originator of this view (about A.D. 325), which reduced Jesus Christ (and the Spirit) below the level of strict deity.[11] He admitted that Christ existed before the foundation of the world, but he denied that He was coeternal with the Father. Arius, by teaching that the Spirit was brought into existence by the Son, reduced Him to a lesser form of deity.

In more recent times, some movements, such as Unitarianism, Russellism (Jehovah's Witnesses), and Mormonism assign our Lord and the Holy Spirit a nature and position below that of true deity. T.C. Hammond suggests:

> This is one of the most important battlegrounds in the history of the church, and no true Christian should for one moment tolerate any description of our Master other than that which assigns to Him the fullest deity, coequal and coeternal with the Father.[12]

God's Will and Providence

It is also important that we know about God's providence and will if our knowledge of God is to be accurate. He is not only the Creator of the universe and the Triune God, but He is also the physical *Sustainer* of His creation, and the moral *Governor* of the intelligent beings He has created.

The sweep of God's providence and sovereignty are complete and comprehensive. "The Lord does whatever pleases him, in the heavens and on the earth, in the seas and all their depths" (Ps. 135:6). This truth is echoed in the New Testament: "They [the rulers] did what your power and will had decided beforehand should happen" (Acts 4:28). God is the One in whom "all things hold together" (Col. 1:17). He is the One "who works out everything in conformity with the purpose of his will" (Eph. 1:11).

God's Eternal Plan

God's control of the universe is often spoken of in terms of His *decrees*. By the decrees of God we mean "that eternal plan by which God makes sure that all the events of the universe—past, present, and future—take place."[13]

To our human, finite minds, decrees and control convey some negative and restrictive overtones. Seeing them from the Creator's all-wise, loving plan, however, puts decrees and control in a different light. They become our safety. With God there is no time as we know it. God exists totally apart from the universe, and yet can be everywhere within it. Time (for the universe) has a beginning. God's existence and activity precede this created time.[14] "In the beginning God created the heavens and the earth" (Gen. 1:1). "By him all things were created: things in heaven and on earth. . . . He is before all things" (Col. 1:16-17).

To God, everything happens in one eternal moment. From this vantage point we view in awe His wisdom and trustworthiness in all He

> **Be assured, God is not about to shortchange us in life. The complete opposite is true.**

does. This is why we say *God knows the end from the beginning.*

When we think about God's will, we must consider these truths:

• God's absolute *decrees* are always accomplished (i.e., natural laws, the creation of the universe, and the creation in God's image of the human race with a free will).

• People may disobey God's *purposes* for His creatures (i.e., Adam in the Garden of Eden). We turn from His purposes when we choose to sin. God gave His decrees so that His created ones could have optimal life. We may ignore His purposes because we were not created automatons. We have responsibility for our individual lives and what we do with them.

God has given His human creatures the dignity and the compliment of choice, as C.S. Lewis describes it.

• God's directive will is what He brings to pass.

• God's permissive will is what He allows to take place.

God *permitted*, but did not *direct*, the entrance of sin into the world. But whether actively (by decree) or passively (by permission), God is sovereign over all that happens. God is *free* in that He is under no other influence or power of anything or anyone but Himself. "Who has understood the mind of the Lord, or instructed him as his counselor?" (Isa.

40:13) He is *sovereign*—He has power to bring His divine decrees to succeess.

What about Free Will?

The statement "God is sovereign over all that happens," raises some big questions. If God directs everything, how can people be free agents and therefore morally responsible? If God knows in advance what people are going to do, then, what choice do they have in the matter? Admittedly, there are profound aspects to this question that are not altogether clear, but it is helpful to keep several things in mind.

• First, *a person's will is always a relatively small part of any given circumstance.* People have no control over when or where they are born or the abilities, disabilities, advantages, or disadvantages they are given at birth. They are subject to many influences beyond their control. We are all rather like a baby in a playpen who has real freedom, but only within certain prescribed bounds. Francis Schaeffer points out that when someone throws a man a ball, he can either catch it or let it fall. Barring some physical defect, he is not so limited that he has no power of decision or choice. But he does have some prohibitions. He can't make the ball fly up in the air!

• Second, *God's foreknowledge is not in itself the cause of what happens.* For example, God foreknew that Demas would forsake the Apostle Paul for love of this world, but God's foreknowledge did not *predispose* Demas to turn back, much less *compel* him to do so. Demas acted in freedom; he made his own personal choice, under no compulsion (2 Tim. 4:10).

Again, God foreknew that Saul would receive Christ and become Paul the Apostle, but on the Damascus Road, Saul exercised his own will in answering the Lord's summons (Acts 9). God foreknows your decisions before you make them—He knows what you will do and where you will go—but this foreknowledge does not interfere in the slightest with your complete freedom to act.

J.I. Packer calls this difficulty (reconciling divine sovereignty and human freedom) an *antinomy,* an apparent contradiction between conclusions that seem equally logical, reasonable, or necessary. He explains:

Modern physics faces an antinomy, in this sense, in its study of light. There is cogent evidence to show that light consists of waves, and equally cogent evidence to show that it consists of particles. It is not apparent how light can be both waves and particles, but the evidence is there, and so neither view can be ruled out in favor of the other.[15]

The sovereignty of God and the free will of man may appear on the surface to be irreconcilable. Nevertheless, both exist. We may take comfort that divine sovereignty is exercised by a *trustworthy, all-loving, all-knowing* God. Also, His sovereignty in no way lessens our freedom—or our privilege and responsibility to know and do His good will. Increased knowledge of Him brings out deep trust and unbridled worship at every turn of life.

Deuteronomy tells us aptly: "For the Lord your God is God of gods and Lord of lords, the great God, mighty and awesome. . . . Fear the Lord your God and serve him. Hold fast to him and take your oaths in his name. He is your praise; he is your God" (10:17, 20-21).

Jesus Christ

D r. W.H. Griffith Thomas wrote a book entitled *Christianity Is Christ*. This title sums up the heart and uniqueness of Christianity.

Buddha is not essential to the teaching of Buddhism, or Muhammad to Islam, but everything about Christianity is determined by the person and work of Jesus Christ. Christianity owes its life, substance, and character in every detail to Christ. He was:

the author of its teachings,
the object of its doctrine,
the origin of its salvation,
the fulfillment of its hopes,
the source of its power,
the founder of its church, and
the one who gave the Holy Spirit as a legacy to those who believe.

But who is this Man, Jesus Christ? His identity was the central emphasis of His ministry. He asked a disciple, Peter, "Who do you say I am?" (Matt. 16:15) This is the pivotal question of Christianity as the history of the church has shown.

Fully God

The unalterable foundation of Christianity is: *Jesus Christ was fully God.* He is expressly called God in numerous passages of Scripture. One example is John 1:1: "The Word was God" (*Word* refers to Jesus). John 1:14 also states, "The Word became flesh and lived for a while among us." Other scriptural passages also refer to Jesus as God, including: "our great God and Savior, Jesus Christ" (Titus 2:13), and "his Son Jesus Christ. . . the true God and eternal life" (1 John 5:20) At His birth He was named "Jesus," the Greek form of Joshua, meaning "God saves." At His baptism, He was called the "Messiah" and the Christ.

Jesus is not man becoming God, but God incarnate coming into human flesh, coming into it from the outside. His life is the highest and the holiest entering in at the lowliest door.[1]

Jesus Christ Claimed Deity

Jesus claimed deity for Himself in a way quite clear to His listeners. He said, on one occasion, "I and the Father [God] are one" (John 10:30). His decisive expression of deity was considered by the religious leaders to be blasphemy and eventually led to His crucifixion: "The Jews insisted, 'We have a law, and according to that law he must die, because he claimed to be the Son of God' " (John 19:7). The high priest expressly asked Christ, "Tell us if you are the Christ, the Son of God." Jesus answered, "Yes, it is as you say" (Matt. 26:63-64).

This straightforward, affirmative answer brought the high priest to declare there was no further need of other witnesses. They had heard Jesus' "blasphemy" with their own ears. He had said for all to hear that "God [was] his own Father, making himself equal with God" (John 5:18).

Displayed God's Authority

Jesus Christ claimed the prerogatives and authority of God. He said He had authority to *forgive sins* (Mark 2:10), and He said He would *come on the clouds of heaven and sit at the right hand of the Mighty One* (Mark 14:62).

Implying authority to *judge men*, He said, "The Father judges no one, but has entrusted all judgment to the Son" (John 5:22). Several times Jesus asserted that He Himself had the authority and power to *raise the dead* (John 6:39-40, 54; 10:17-18).

Possessed God's Attributes

Jesus demonstrated for all to see and hear the attributes which belong to God alone. He claimed *omnipotence* (all power) with the bold words: "All authority in heaven and on earth has been given to me" (Matt. 28:18). During His life He demonstrated *power over nature* by stilling the stormy waves (Mark 4:39) and turning water into wine (John 2:7-11). He also demonstrated His *power over physical disease* (Mark 3:10), *power over demons* (Luke 4:35), and *power over death* by raising Lazarus from the grave (John 11:43-44). Ephesians 1:19-21 describes His *"incomparably great power. . . . in heavenly realms, far above all rule and authority, power and dominion"* (italics added).

God's qualities were openly displayed in Jesus. He was *omniscient* (all-knowing), knowing as only God could know. He knew what was in men's minds before they spoke (Mark 2:8; John 2:25). He was *omnipresent* (everywhere), and by His Spirit He promised to be with all His disciples to the end of the age (Matt. 28:20).

He Is the Center

John and others describe Jesus as the Creator: "Through him all things were made; without him nothing was made that has been made" (John 1:3). He is also called the Sustainer of the universe (Heb. 1:3). Perhaps the most comprehensive statement about the deity of Christ is this: "In Christ all the fullness of the Deity lives in bodily form" (Col. 2:9).

As Creator-God, Jesus Christ was "preexistent" with the Father. He did not *become* the Son of God either at His *birth* or sometime during His earthly life. He *was* and *is* the eternal Son, coexistent and coeternal with the Father. In a conversation with some who were against Him, Jesus remarked that Abraham rejoiced to see His coming. The Jews were dumbfounded, "You are not yet fifty years old . . . and you have seen Abraham?" He replied, "I tell you the truth, before Abraham was born, I am!" (See John 8:57-58.) Of course, He existed before Abraham since He was the *Creator!*

Jesus Christ *accepted worship* from men due only to God. He commended rather than rebuked doubting Thomas, who fell at His feet and declared in awe, "My Lord and my God!" (John 20:28) This was the same Jesus who scorned Satan's invitation to worship him by replying, "Worship the Lord your God, and serve him only" (Matt. 4:10; see also Deut. 6:13).

The deity of Christ is woven into the warp and woof of everything He said and did! Those who heard Him understood and confirmed His claim to be one with God. The things He did were affirming evidence that His words were *not* clever deceit or the babblings of a demented person.

He Was Fully Man

Jesus was not only fully God—He was also fully man, fully human. This is a vital aspect of the person of Christ. If He were not fully human, He could not have represented us on the cross. Also, He could not be the High Priest who comforts and strengthens us. As a man, He has gone through our human experience (Heb. 2:16-18), and He is fully able *to understand and sympathize with us.* That is an astonishing truth.

Though His conception was supernatural, Jesus' birth was that of a normal child born of a human mother (Matt. 1:18). He is spoken of as being born of the seed of the woman (Gen. 3:15) and of the seed of Abraham (Heb. 2:16, KJV). In this way, through the virgin birth, "the Word became flesh" (John 1:14). Jesus, as a normal child, grew physically and mentally: "And the child grew and became strong; he was filled with wisdom, and the grace of God was upon him" (Luke 2:40).

Jesus referred to Himself as a man: "As it is, you are determined to kill me, a man who has told you the truth that I heard from God" (John 8:40). Others recognized Him as a man. (See Acts 2:22.) He had a body, soul, and spirit, and shared our physical and emotional experiences.

- Jesus got hungry and thirsty (Matt. 4:2; John 19:28).
- He got weary from traveling (John 4:6).
- He needed sleep and refreshment (Matt. 8:24).
- He experienced and expressed love and compassion (Matt. 9:36).
- He was angry at those who defiled His Father's house (Matt. 21:13).
- He denounced those who refused the truth of God (Mark 3:5).

• He wept at the tomb of a dear friend (John 11:35).
• He was troubled within as He faced the cross (John 12:27).

"The Son of Man"

In the Gospels Jesus called Himself the "Son of Man" eighty times. Though He claimed attributes of deity, at the same time He asserted His identification with *us* as sons of men by using this title. Although first used of an apocalyptic figure in Daniel 7:13, Jesus used the phrase "the Son of Man" frequently of Himself, specifically stating He was the one coming to give His life as a ransom for many (Mark 10:45).

Jesus' humanity was unique in that it was *complete*. Our Lord, as a man, according to A.H. Strong, was "free from both hereditary depravity and from actual sin, as is shown by His never offering sacrifice, never praying for [His own] forgiveness, teaching that all but He needed the new birth, challenging the dissenters to convict Him of a single sin."[2]

Christ's humanity was as real and genuine as His deity. We must maintain belief in both, emphasizing neither at the expense of the other.

Mostly Man or Mostly God?

A brief review of church history will illustrate how easy it is to emphasize one aspect of Christ's nature over the other. Some of these tendencies are with us today and need to be recognized. Heresies forced the early church to define the truth clearly. This review will give a sketch of the

HIS BIRTH SPLIT TIME IN TWO

Two thousand years ago the birth of Jesus Christ rocked the world. His birth changed its calendar and tailored its mores. The atheist dates his checks with 1999, declaring Christ's birth. The rulers of countries both east and west, regardless of their religions, use His birth date. Unthinkingly, we declare His birth on letters, legal documents, and datebooks.

main deviations.

• The Ebionites, early in the second century, *denied the deity* of Christ. They maintained He was merely a man, though supernaturally conceived and having a peculiar relationship to God.

• The Docetists, later in the same century, *denied Jesus' true humanity,* rejecting the reality of His human body as merely a phantom appearing to be human. Jesus' life on earth, they held, was largely an illusion. They even implied the divine Christ was not hungry or thirsty, nor did He suffer and die.

• The Arians, forerunners of today's Unitarians (*accepting the moral teachings but rejecting the divinity of Jesus*), mistook the biblical statements about Christ's subordination to the Father as teaching His inferiority. Christ was somehow created by the Father as the first and highest being, but not as God. This belief is current today in several major cults.

• The Apollinarians were condemned at the Council of Constantinople in A.D. 381. Heavily influenced by Greek philosophy, Apollinarius taught that Christ had a true body and soul but the *human mind was replaced by His divine being.* This view implied that Jesus was not fully human and therefore not tempted in every respect as we are.

• Nestorius, in the fifth century, emphasized the distinctness of Christ's two natures and *denied a real union between the divine and human* Jesus. He made this union a moral one rather than an organic one. Nestorians virtually believed in two natures and two persons instead of *two* natures in *one* person.

• The Eutychians, at the opposite extreme, *denied two distinctive natures.* They said the divine and the human natures in Christ were absorbed or "merged" into a third sort of nature, particular to Christ. This group was condemned as heretical at the Council of Chalcedon in A.D. 451.

Both Human and Divine

The question of the two natures of Christ is obviously complex, with numerous subtleties. The Chalcedon Council summed up the orthodox view succinctly, making four helpful points.

In the one person, Jesus Christ,

1. there are two natures, a human nature and a divine nature,

2. each has its completeness and integrity, and

3. these two natures are organically and indissolubly united, so no third nature is formed thereby.

4. In brief, orthodox doctrine forbids us either to divide the person or confound the natures.[3]

JESUS	
Fully God	**Fully Man**
All-knowing	Angry
All-powerful	Hungry, thirsty, tired
Calmed the storm	Loved His disciples
Coexistent with the Father	Tempted by Satan
Creator	Troubled within
Healed the sick	Suffered
Rose from the dead	Wept

In an attempt to comprehend Christ's two natures, some have suggested various "kenosis" theories. *Kenosis* comes from the Greek word *kenoo*, meaning "emptied." It was taken from Philippians 2:7: "He made himself nothing" or "emptied himself" as the *Revised Standard Version* puts it. Some contended this meant Christ totally emptied Himself of deity. Others held He still somehow possessed His divine attributes, but He renounced them.

T.C. Hammond explains: "our Lord's attributes of deity were *at no time laid aside*. Any 'explanation' of His divine-human nature which violates the integrity of His deity is obviously to be rejected."[4]

The deity and humanity of Christ's one person is admittedly a profound subject. We know by revelation that it is true, thus we can readily accept this mystery. The early church creeds did not try to explain this

TITLES OF JESUS CHRIST

Jesus: Greek form of the Hebrew, Joshua, "the Lord saves"
Christ: "The anointed one"—Greek—used in N.T.
Messiah: "The anointed one"—Hebrew—also used for priests
King of the Jews: King Herod's name for Jesus
Lord and Savior Jesus Christ
Son of God, Son of Man
Lamb of God
Teacher, Rabbi, Shepherd, Ruler, etc.
Savior, the Lord

mystery but found acceptable a terse affirmation rather than a full explanation. This has been used ever since. Athanasius said: "He became what He was not; He continued to be what He was."

In an effort to eliminate the difficulties that arise from the problem of Christ's two natures, some theologians go to one of two extremes. Some exalt Christ's human nature to a level that would separate Him from the rest of humanity. For example, they say His nature was that of unfallen Adam. For this, there is no evidence in the Gospel records of His earthly life. Others, on the other hand, water down His deity. This view makes our Lord, on earth, subject to all human limitations—with, of course, the exception of sin.

"The fact that is forgotten, and may well be the only key to the problem, is the ministry of the Holy Spirit in the person and life of Christ," writes R.A. Finlayson. He continues:

That Spirit, who had prepared His humanity and kept the unborn Child free from the taint of a mother's sin, never left Him, but throughout all the temptations and sufferings of His life and death brought to His human soul the light and comfort and strength which He needed to accomplish His task. In the light of that gracious ministry, we can understand, in some measure, how the divine nature was acting under human conditions, and how the human nature was acting in the fullest unity with the divine. That Spirit, who shared the eternal counsels of the Godhead, unified the consciousness of Christ so that there could be no possibility of division or dualism within Him. For this reason we can understand how there was nothing unnatural or inhuman about the self-consciousness of Jesus, even when He was in unbroken communion with the supernatural and eternal.

"However we explain it . . . saving faith has always reached out to One who is perfect man, true God, the one Christ. In the strength and fellowship of this faith we, as Christians, are called to abide."[5]

A proper knowledge of Christ's person is crucial in understanding His work. If He were not the God-man, His work could not have eternal and personal significance for us. There is no more succinct and clear explanation of Jesus Christ's coming than an early Christian hymn in Philippians 2:6-11.

He had the very nature of God.
He made Himself nothing.
He humbled Himself.
He became obedient to death.
He even went to death on a cross.

"Therefore God exalted Him to the highest place and gave Him the name that is above every name, that at the name of Jesus every knee should bow, in heaven and on earth and under the earth, and every tongue confess that Jesus Christ is Lord, to the glory of God the Father."

This is the Bible's answer to "Who is Jesus Christ?"

While fully appreciating who Jesus *is*, of equal importance is understanding what He has *done*—and is doing—for all who will believe. If Jesus had not been fully God, He *could not* be our Savior from sin. On the other hand, if He were God and yet did nothing on our behalf—that is, did not *do* something to bring us to God—He *would* not be our Savior. Jesus not only *could* save men—He did.

A Perfect Man

Christ was the perfect man. As such, He was without sin in thought, word, or deed. He was able to challenge His enemies with the question "Can any of you prove me guilty of sin?" (John 8:46) His foes had no reply. He was totally obedient to the Father. He said, "My food is to do the will of him who sent me and to finish his work" (John 4:34).

There are three reasons why our Lord's perfect life was a necessity.

1. It qualified Him to become the sacrificial offering for sin. Old Testament types all insist on the purity of the offering given for sacrifice.

2. It meant that perfect obedience was rendered to God, in contrast to Adam's disobedience. Scripture emphasizes this repeatedly (Rom. 5:19; Heb. 10:6-7).

3. Through His obedience, Jesus became a qualified Mediator and High Priest for His people (Heb. 2:11-18).

Jesus Christ was, par excellence, "a Man with a mission." He knew what was ahead for Him. He frequently said, at a point of crisis, "My time has *not yet* come" (John 2:4, italics added; see also John 7:6). Finally, He said, "The hour *has come* for the Son of Man to be glorified" (John 12:23, italics added). A little later, as He contemplated the awfulness of the cross, He said, "Now my heart is troubled, and what shall I say? 'Father, save me from this hour?' " (John 12:27) The reason He had come, as He had said, was to "seek and to save what was lost" (Luke 19:10) and to "give his life as a ransom for many" (Mark 10:45). So central is the death of Christ to an understanding of Christianity that we will discuss it more fully in a later chapter.

Whimpering Men into Roaring Lions

Not only did Jesus Christ live and die, but the triumphant dynamic of Christianity is that He also *rose from the dead.* The common greeting of the early church was the dramatic reminder "He is risen!" It was the thing that changed a handful of cowardly, whimpering men, who denied that they even knew their leader, into roaring lions (Matt. 26:70, 72, 74). It was the fact that they had seen Jesus alive from the dead that changed them. Then they proclaimed boldly the truth of the Resurrection. Peter, at the risk of his life, just fifty days after the Resurrection, declared in Jerusalem: "God has raised this Jesus to life, and we are all witnesses of the fact" (Acts 2:32).

Both the death and the resurrection of Christ show His supremacy and His uniqueness among all the religious leaders of the world.

A number of times Jesus predicted both His death and His resurrection (Mark 8:31; 10:32-34; see also Matt. 16:21). But such a statement was so fantastic that the disciples didn't believe it until they had the firsthand evidence of seeing Him themselves after His entombment.

It is important to understand that the resurrection of Christ was a *bodily* resurrection, not one of "spirit" or "influence," as some suggest. The disciples, on first seeing Jesus after He rose, thought they were seeing a ghost and were terribly frightened. Jesus had to say to them, "Look at my hands and my feet. It is I myself! Touch me and see; a ghost does not have flesh and bones, as you see I have" (Luke 24:39). He proceeded to eat fish and honey with them to further demonstrate His physical reality. Ghosts don't eat fish!

He invited doubting Thomas to put his finger in the nail prints and put his hand in the pierced side (John 20:27), so giving further testimony to the physical nature of his resurrect body and also indicating that this was the body that had been crucified and buried.

Jesus' resurrection body, however, differed from our bodies and from His own previous body. For instance, our risen Lord passed through closed doors when He met with the disciples for the first time in the Upper Room (John 20:19). Paul discusses at some length the subject of the Resurrection and the resurrection body (1 Cor. 15). This passage should be studied carefully.

Resurrection: Fact, Not Fiction

Many attempts have been made to explain away the Resurrection. This chapter cannot contain a full discussion of the subject.

Some false theories of the Resurrection (such as the swoon theory) revolve around denial of Christ's actual death. Other views hold that the disciples made an honest error which led them sincerely but wrongly to proclaim that Jesus had risen from the dead.

But all attempts to explain away the Resurrection flounder on the rocks of the actual evidence. Christ would have been a deceiver had He only *swooned* and allowed the disciples to think He had actually risen from the dead. The disciples were not prepared for a *hallucination*. They didn't *expect* He *would* rise, and they didn't *believe* He *had* risen from the dead. They had to be persuaded against their "better judgment" that it was so (Luke 24:36-45). Furthermore, Christ *appeared ten times*, in ten different places, and in one case to more than 500 people at once. Such an event cannot be explained by a "hallucination." Also, the disciples would have been deceivers if they had stolen Christ's body. Nearly all of them died for their faith as martyrs. People will die for what they *mistak-*

enly think is true, but they don't die for what they *know is false*. The inability of the enemies of Christ to produce His body is further evidence that it had not been stolen.

The *empty tomb*, the revolutionized lives of the disciples, the Lord's Day (worship being shifted from Saturday to Sunday because of the Resurrection), the existence of the Christian church (which can be traced back to approximately A.D. 30)—all are conclusive evidence that the Resurrection is fact, not fiction.

The final evidence is the *transformed lives* of countless people today who have met and been given new life by the risen Christ.

Four Resurrection Benefits to Us

The implications of the Resurrection are enormous. We should understand them as fully as possible—and *enjoy* them.

1. First, as we have seen, the Resurrection fully confirms the *truth and validity* of what Jesus taught and did. Paul says, "And if Christ has not been raised, your faith is futile; you are still in your sins" (1 Cor. 15:17). Because of the Resurrection, we know we are not trusting in a myth; we know that our sins are actually forgiven through the death of Christ. Certainty and forgiveness are based on the empty tomb! Christ is the only one who has ever come back from death to tell men about the beyond. In *His* words we know we have the authoritative Word of God Himself.

2. Second, Christ's resurrection is the guarantee of *our own resurrection.* Jesus said, "Because I live, you also will live" (John 14:19). We know with assurance that the grave is not our end and that we shall be raised as He was.

3. Third, we know that *the body is in itself good,* not inherently evil, as some have mistakenly thought. The fact that our Lord became flesh and took a physical body in the Incarnation shows this. It is confirmed by the Resurrection, which tells us that in the eternal state, body and soul will be reunited, though the body will, of course, be a glorified body like our Lord's. Christ is the one "who . . . will transform our lowly bodies so that they will be like His glorious body" (Phil. 3:21).

4. Fourth, we have assurance of the *contemporary power of Christ* in life today. We do not believe in a dead Christ hanging on a cross or lying in a grave, but in the risen Christ of the empty tomb. Christ gives us His life in salvation. This is the contemporary power, the dynamic, of Christian faith.

Jesus' Ascension and Exaltation

Jesus not only predicted His death and resurrection, but He also predicted His ascension and exaltation (John 6:62; 17:1). In the Ascension, He visibly left His disciples and the earth and returned to heaven, forty days after His resurrection. His exit from this life was as miraculous as His entrance. The account of it is given in Acts 1:9-11.

Having ascended, Christ is now seated at the right hand of the Father in heaven, "far above all rule and authority, power and dominion, and every title that can be given" (Eph. 1:20-21). His ascension and exaltation were necessary for the completion of His work of redemption. As the ascended and exalted Christ, He has entered heaven as a forerunner for us (Heb. 6:20), making our entrance possible. Believers will follow Him because His atoning sacrifice has been applied to them.

Now before God, He is our High Priest and Advocate, and "appears for us in God's presence" (Heb. 9:24; see also 1 Tim. 2:5). His sacrificial work is accomplished and His advocacy for us is unceasing. "If anybody does sin, we have one who speaks to the Father in our defense—Jesus Christ, the Righteous One" (1 John 2:1). As our Mediator or Advocate (*King James Version*), Christ is now active for us before the throne of God.

He Gives Us Free Access to God

Christ also ascended to prepare a place for us in heaven. He clearly told the disciples, "I will come back and take you to be with me that you also may be where I am" (John 14:3). All Christians should look forward with deep anticipation to the return of their Lord for them.

Because of the ascension and exaltation of Christ, we have free and confident access into the very presence of God. We can "approach the throne of grace with confidence" (Heb. 4:16). In Old Testament times, access to the presence of God was limited to one person—the high priest; to one place—the holy of holies in the tabernacle (or the temple); and to one time—the Day of Atonement. Because Christ is our High Priest in heaven, *each of us has access to the Creator* at *any* time and at *any* place. How the angels must wonder that we make so little use of this privilege of audience with the King!

Christianity is Christ from beginning to end. To know who Jesus Christ is and what He has done is to increase our awe, wonder, and appreciation of the One who, "though he was rich, yet for your sakes he became poor, so that you through his poverty might become rich" (2 Cor. 8:9).

Jesus Christ's Death

The cross of Jesus Christ has been called "the central fact of human history." To the entire world the cross is the primary symbol of Christianity; it crowns church spires, highlights church auditoriums, and even dangles on jewelry counters.

This spotlight on the cross declares God's planned purpose for the coming of Jesus Christ into human history. For both God and our world, the cross carries monumental significance, "the weight of glory," as C.S. Lewis expressed it in his book of the same name. It was the climactic fulfillment of God's covenant, His design to close the gap between Himself and humanity.

Jesus Himself said the cross was His intentional, redemptive goal. "The Son of Man did not come to be served, but to serve, and to give his life as a ransom for many" (Mark 10:45). "The Son of Man came to seek and to save what was lost" (Luke 19:10).

The death of Christ on the cross also singles out the "uniqueness" of Christianity. Here God has done for us what we cannot do for ourselves. He has provided the way for each one of us, prone to sin and distant from our Maker, to be forgiven and brought into vital relationship with Him. All this is based not on something we must *do*, but on something God Himself in His Son has already *done*.

Every other religious system in the world is essentially a *"do-it your-self"* proposition. Only in Christianity is salvation a free gift, not because we deserve it, but prompted by the incomprehensible goodness of God's love. It is true, the cross of Christ is the central fact of human history.

> **The cross is the only ladder high enough to reach heaven.**
>
> **Jesus was crucified not in a cathedral between two candles but on a cross between two thieves.**

When we grasp the full meaning Christ's death has for us, we can enthusiastically join all creation and declare He is worthy to receive our worship (Rev. 5:9, 12-13).

Forecast in the Old Testament

Christ's death is the central theme of both Old and New Testaments. As far back as the Garden of Eden, when God cursed the serpent, He promised victory over evil and a Deliverer (Gen. 3:15). The Prophet Isaiah gives us a clear promise of One who would die for our sins. "But he was pierced for our transgressions, he was crushed for our iniquities; the punishment that brought us peace was upon him, and by his wounds we are healed. We all, like sheep, have gone astray, each of us has turned to his own way; and the Lord has laid on him the iniquity of us all" (Isa. 53:5-6).

Jesus Himself spoke of the Old Testament prophecies declaring He would suffer. He specifically said, "These are the Scriptures that testify about me" (John 5:39; 12:41). God's plan for deliverance was built on the sacrificial system; He instituted the blood sacrifice. Final deliverance came with Christ's sacrifice, explained this way in Hebrews: "When this priest [Jesus] had offered for *all time one sacrifice for sins*, he sat down at the right hand of God" (Heb. 10:12, italics added). Jesus accomplished what the Old Testament priests could only hope for.

These prophets, who lived from 700 to 500 B.C., were writing about these events without knowing firsthand who Christ was or when He would come. According to 1 Peter 1:10-12 they were writing for others who would read their message later. They were writing for us today.

The death of Christ is linked to the Old Testament covenant when God first announced to Abram: "All peoples on earth will be blessed through you" (Gen. 12:3). After that, God repeatedly unfolded Himself and His promise throughout Israel's history. Two factors underlie His plan.

Mankind's persistent bent toward sin separates each of us from an infinitely holy God: "But your iniquities have separated you from your God; your sins have hidden his face from you, so that he will not hear" (Isa. 59:2). God, in mercy, takes the initiative and provides the way by which our estrangement can be ended.

The first record of man and woman sinning is followed by a need for covering. Adam said, "I was afraid because I was naked" (Gen. 3:10), that is, "I am no longer innocent," and God provided animal skins to cover him and Eve. Then Cain and Abel are recorded as bringing an "offering" to the Lord. The idea of sacrifice was divinely revealed and directed toward the goal of personal holiness, reconciliation with God.

Leon Morris comments, "In the Old Testament, [forgiveness] is usually said to be obtained by the sacrifices, but it must never be forgotten that God says of the atoning blood, 'I have given it to you'"[1] (Lev. 17:11). Atonement is secured by sacrifice, the divinely appointed way of securing atonement.

The Sacrificial System

The whole sacrificial system of the Old Testament was a symbolic portrayal to be fulfilled in Christ. The Passover, celebrated at the time of the Exodus of enslaved Israelites from Egypt, is the fullest picture of Christ's sacrifice. Each believing family slew a perfect lamb and put its blood on the doorposts and lintels of the house. The angel of death, when he saw the blood, passed over that household. Those believers then escaped the judgment of having their firstborn die. As with other sacrifices, the elements of the perfection of the lamb, the shedding of blood, and substitution were all present.

Christ was the fulfillment of all that the Passover lamb stood for. He was "the Lamb of God, who takes away the sin of the world" (John 1:29). Those who in faith offered animal sacrifices in Old Testament times looked forward to the coming Messiah, just as we by faith look back to

Central Fact of History

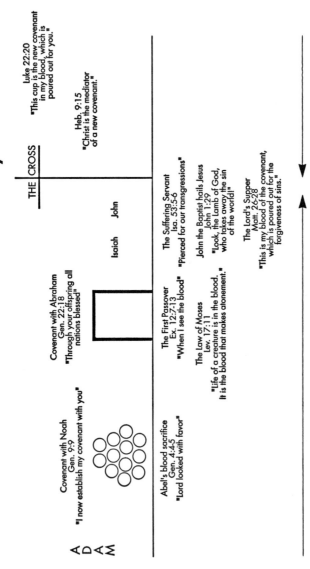

THE CROSS

Luke 22:20
"This cup is the new covenant
in my blood, which is
poured out for you."

Heb. 9:15
"Christ is the mediator
of a new covenant."

Isaiah   John

Covenant with Abraham
Gen. 22:18
"Through your offspring all
nations blessed"

Covenant with Noah
Gen. 9:9
"I now establish my covenant with you"

A
D
A
M

The Suffering Servant
Isa. 53:5-6
"Pierced for our transgressions"

John the Baptist hails Jesus
John 1:29
"Look, the Lamb of God,
who takes away the sin
of the world!"

The Lord's Supper
Matt. 26-28
"This is my blood of the covenant,
which is poured out for the
forgiveness of sins."

The First Passover
Ex. 12:7-13
"When I see the blood"

The Law of Moses
Lev. 17:11
"Life of a creature is in the blood.
It is the blood that makes atonement."

Abel's blood sacrifice
Gen. 4:4-5
"Lord looked with favor"

Heb. 10:14
"By one sacrifice he has made
perfect forever those who
are being made holy."

Rom. 3:26
"Just and the one who justifies"

the cross of Christ. The animal sacrifices did not save, but faith in what they symbolized *did*. We by faith see Jesus as the fulfillment of the symbols. As Isaac Watts wrote:

> Not all the blood of beasts
> On Jewish altars slain
> Could give the guilty conscience peace,
> Or wash away the stain.
> But Christ the heavenly Lamb
> Takes all our sins away;
> A sacrifice of nobler name
> And richer blood than they.

Christ's Death in the New Testament

The remedy for sin, a sacrifice or penalty, continues to be the central theme of the New Testament. In the New Testament, writers use several terms to explain the significance of Christ's excruciating crucifixion.

• Christ's death is spoken of as the *atonement* for our sin. It has been suggested that *atonement* means, basically, "at-one-ment"—that is to say, a bringing together of those who are estranged. But the Old Testament word means, essentially, "to cover." The animal sacrifices provided a "covering" for sin until the death of Christ would forever destroy sin's power. In the New Testament, various ideas explain and illustrate the Atonement.

• The Atonement is spoken of as a *reconciliation*: "When we were God's enemies, we were reconciled to him [God] through the death of his Son" (Rom. 5:10; see also 2 Cor. 5:18-19; Eph. 2:16; Col. 1:20). Reconciliation implies former hostility between the reconciled parties. Sin separates us from a holy God. The death of Christ did away with the cause of God's enmity by taking away our sin. We have been reconciled to God, the root cause of alienation having been removed. God has always loved us, and still loves us. But His wrath—a fixed, permanent attitude against evil—has been turned away from us. He sees us as reconciled through Christ.

• *Appeasement* or *propitiation* are also used to describe the atoning death of Christ. Propitiation is used only in the *King James Version*, but it carries the same idea. Both of these words have within them the concept of "the removal of wrath by the offering of a gift," as Morris wrote.[2] "God presented him as a sacrifice of atonement, through faith in his blood. He did this to demonstrate his justice, because in his forbearance he had left the sins committed beforehand unpunished" (Rom. 3:25).

These terms have a personal quality to them. A young man might appease his girlfriend, for example, by sending her a bouquet of roses. This carries the idea of a restored relationship. Jesus, in this case, laid down His life for us, fully and perfectly satisfying God's holy and just standards. It could be said Jesus *appeased* God's wrath against evil.

• *Ransom*, the word used by Jesus Himself to define His death, is closely linked to the idea of redemption—buying back or restoring. "[Christ] gave himself a ransom for all man—the testimony given in its proper time" (1 Tim. 2:6; see also 1 Peter 1:18). *Ransom* was commonly used in Greek to refer to the price paid for redeeming a slave, that is the price paid to release a slave from bondage. Through His death, Jesus paid the price to free us all from the enslavement of sin. We are redeemed, set free. "You know that it was not with perishable things such as silver or gold that you were redeemed . . . but with the precious blood of Christ, a lamb without blemish or defect" (1 Peter 1:18-19).

God does not first reconcile us, ransom us, and then love us. Rather, because He loves us, He opens the way for reconciliation, appeasement, and ransom.

Our Substitute

Among the various terms that give the clearest explanations of the death of Christ is the word *substitute*. "Christ died for sins once for all, the righteous for the unrighteous, to bring you to God" (1 Peter 3:18). Christ died for *us*—that is, in our place. "God made him who had no sin to be sin for us, so that in him we might become the righteousness of God" (2 Cor. 5:21). The whole concept of sacrifice for sin carries with it the idea of substitution, which is fulfilled in Christ, who "bore our sins in his body on the tree, so that we might die to sins and live for righteousness; by his wounds you have been healed" (1 Peter 2:24).

Suppose a man were sentenced to pay a large fine and serve a prison sentence. If the judge were his friend, and loved the man so much that he took off his robes and served the sentence for the man, he would be his substitute. The man himself could go free, uncondemned. The weight of his sentence would be on his friend, the judge.

This illustration is somewhat inadequate, but it may give a slight insight into how God, the Creator, laid aside His deity and paid our ransom, reconciling us by becoming our substitute. The teaching that Christ has taken our place and suffered and died in our behalf runs clearly throughout the Gospels and the rest of the New Testament.

There is no ambiguity in God's intention throughout the Bible. From the very beginning of creation His desire is to have a relationship with those whom He created. Reconciliation, ransom, and sacrifice are all the result of God's unceasing desire to bring each one of us close to Himself.

Attempts to Minimize Christ's Death

Throughout history many people have tried to discredit or discount Christ's death on the cross. Following are the most prominent theories and objections.

1. The *moral influence* or *example* theory states that man needs only to repent and reform to be reconciled to God. Advocates of this view believe the death of Christ was merely a powerful example, and we are redeemed as we allow His example to have a determining influence on our own efforts at moral improvement.

There is, of course, great moral influence in Christ's example. It is true that "Christ suffered for you, leaving you an example, that you should follow in his steps" (1 Peter 2:21). Scripture unmistakably teaches not only that sin has defiled us personally, *but also* that we are guilty before a holy God. Many Scriptures are unequivocal about Christ coming to die *for our sins.* The moral influence theory ignores these passages entirely.

2. The *governmental* theory holds that Christ's death was necessary to preserve God's divine law and authority with "some exhibition of the high estimate which God places upon His law and on the heinous guilt of violating it."[3] But why is *Christ* necessary, if this is all there is to His public sacrifice? And why should One who is *perfect* suffer, rather than one who is *guilty?*

It is true that the cross shows vividly the destructive nature of sin, and it is an eloquent testimony that man may not ignore or toy with the Law of God. In this view, sacrifice is surely not congruent with the Apostle

Paul's words, "God made him [Jesus] who had no sin to be sin for us so that in him we might become the righteousness of God" (2 Cor. 5:21). Also, this view fails in view of the Scriptures already referred to.

3. An *accident of history,* unexpected and unforeseen, is another proposal for Christ's death that Scripture does not support. Christ Himself assured His disciples that it was for this purpose that He had come into the world (John 12:27). In the Garden of Gethsemane, He prayed to His Heavenly Father, "Yet not as I will, but as you will" (Matt. 26:39). Jesus sums it up: "The reason my Father loves me is that I lay down my life—only to take it up again. No one takes it from me, but I lay it down of my own accord. I have authority to lay it down and authority to take it up again" (John 10:17-18).

The prophets also predicted the Messiah's sacrificial death and, in fact, all scriptural evidence opposes the idea that Christ's death was accidental. The truth is Christ did not *have* to die, but He *voluntarily* endured the cross for us. This is one of the central and most moving aspects of His sacrifice.

4. That Christ was merely *another martyr* of history has also been suggested. This theory suggests that the gathering storm of political and religious turmoil might have been responsible for Christ's death. If this were the case, how could forgiveness come from His death, and how do we account for Jesus' statement, when He first celebrated "the Lord's Supper"? He stated simply, "This is my blood of the covenant, which is poured out for many for the forgiveness of sins" (Matt. 26:28). A knowledge of Scripture opposes any view of the cross being less than supernatural.

The truth of Jesus Christ dying as our substitute is so prominent throughout the Bible and so awe-inspiring that it can't help but bring us to heartfelt reverence and thanksgiving.

Why Couldn't God Just Forgive?

There have always been some objections to the substitutionary death of Christ. Is not God all-powerful? Is not God all-loving and able to pardon sin without requiring sacrifice? "Why can't He simply forgive sin out of His pure mercy?" skeptics want to know. "Could not an all-powerful God, in His omnipotence, have redeemed the world as easily as He created it?

Since God commands man to forgive freely, why does He Himself not freely forgive?"

This logical question came to Archbishop Anselm in the twelfth century who crystallized the biblical teaching, focusing on forgiveness from God's viewpoint: "God's will is not His own in the sense that anything is permissible to Him or becomes right because He wills it." God cannot deal with sin except as in His holiness He perceives it. If He did not punish it, or make adequate satisfaction for it, then He would be forgiving it unjustly."[4]

Love and Holiness

God's holiness is majestic, undiluted righteousness, and this is our basis for comprehending why we need to be forgiven. We tend to look only at outward acts to judge what is sin. God's view is deeper and less superficial than this; there are no little sins or big sins to a holy God. Holiness means *no* sin. "God looks on the heart." That is where goodness and holiness reside.

God exercises all His attributes in harmony with each other. His holiness demands atonement or, as we call it, a *penalty* for sin. His amazing love provides the payment. God's attributes of love and holiness never violate one another, nor are they antagonistic to each other. They are not in an uneasy equilibrium; rather they work together in full and complete harmony. *Mercy is shown not by trampling upon the claims of justice, but by vicariously satisfying them.*[5]

In the cross of Christ, "Love and faithfulness meet together; righteousness and peace kiss each other" (Ps. 85:10). The New Testament speaks of the "wedding," or coming together, of the attributes of God's love and holiness in the cross of Christ. Through the cross, God can be "just and the one who justifies those who have faith in Jesus" (Rom. 3:26).

In the very act of forgiving sin, or, to use Paul's daring phrase of "justifying the ungodly," God must act in harmony with His whole character. He must show what He is in relation to sin—that evil cannot dwell with Him because He refuses to tolerate sin in any form. In the very process of making forgiveness available to men, of necessity, His complete abhorrence of sin is shown. In other words, God must not merely forgive men, but must forgive in a way which

---

THE CROSS TELLS US:

- Each person is of value to God.
- Iniquity and evil are intolerable to God.
- God's love is deep, His justice is wide, in perfect balance.
- One divine person, Jesus Christ, can pay the debt for the human race.
- Assurance of forgiveness is not presumption, but based on fact.
- We are ransomed, redeemed, restored, renewed.
- The estrangement from our Creator has been healed.
- We can be a child of God, a member of His family.

---

shows that He forever hates evil and can never treat it as other than completely hateful. Sin makes a real difference to God, and even in forgiving, He cannot ignore sin or regard it as other or less than it is. If He did so, He would not be more gracious than He is in the Atonement—He would cease to be God.[6]

Was Christ an Innocent Victim?

Some have alleged that the very idea of God permitting *Christ* to die for *our* sin, as an innocent victim for guilty sinners, was an act of injustice rather than justice. Some even go so far as to call it immoral. But such charges would be true only if Christ were an unwilling victim.

The glory of the cross is in the *voluntary* nature of Christ's coming to earth, keeping in mind He and the Father are *One*. He "did not consider equality with God a thing to be grasped . . . he humbled himself and became obedient to death—even death on a cross" (Phil. 2:6-8). Hammond observes, "The Sufferer must have a double connection between God and Himself on the one hand, and the sinner and Himself on the other."[7]

In considering alternative interpretations, we note that critics may be approaching the doctrine of substitution from preconceived impressions of what God *ought to have done* and from humanistic ethical standards rather than from an understanding of God's character and revelation. On the human level, the substitutionary death of Christ is not an easy concept to comprehend.

One Person Die to Save the Whole World?

How, for example, could the death of one person possibly atone for the innumerable sins of the whole world? From earth's narrow perspective, such atonement would obviously be impossible. One person may die for one other, but for no more than one other. One mass murderer will only pay with his or her life for one of the many people he or she killed.

The effectiveness of the death of Christ depends on *who died*. This was no mere man. Jesus Christ was the God-man: "God was . . . in Christ" (2 Cor. 5:19). Christ's life was of infinite value, and His death likewise had infinite worth. The sum total of the value of all those for whom He died does not approximate the infinite value of Christ's *divine life*, which He surrendered on the cross at Calvary in sacrifice.

Since Christ was only dead for three days, how can His experience be compared with the eternal death millions will experience if they do not trust Him? The "value" of the One who died also answers this question. The death Christ died was an infinite death, both in value and in the intensity of the spiritual suffering the Son of God endured. We simply cannot comprehend what it must have been like for the sinless Son of God to become sin for us (2 Cor. 5:21).

Is it true to say "God died" when Christ died? Robert J. Little points out, in answer to this question, that Christ

> became a man in order to die, for without dying as a man, He could not have delivered men from the penalty of sin. . . . Yet when He died, His *divine being* did not die. And when He died as a man, it was only His body which died. Scripture makes it clear that when *any* human being dies, it is the body which dies. The soul and spirit live on. Hence, when Christ died, we do not say that God died, though He who died on the cross was God. No finite mind can fully understand everything about the infinite God, but we can have some understanding of what is involved.[8]

The Gift of God

A number of clear-cut implications arise from our understanding of the reconciling death of Christ.

One implication is our future destiny—an issue of eternal life or death. The entire Bible is very specific: "The wages of sin is death, but the *gift of God* is eternal life in Christ Jesus our Lord" (Rom. 6:23, italics added). The ravages of sin are knifelike, cutting us apart from God, and bringing moral and spiritual death. Christ's death is God's gift to us, saving us from the consequences of our sin.

The Scripture knows no vagueness about the importance of the cross of Christ. "Whoever believes in the Son *has eternal life,* but whoever rejects the Son *will not see life*" (John 3:36, italics added). There is no in-between ground. A person has either life or death, lives either in light or in darkness, is either saved or lost. Jesus' own words were that He came to "seek and save those who are lost."

Any tendency to hedge on drawing the line between those who are saved and those who are lost cannot be treated lightly. Hedging may be due to our reluctance to appear judgmental or perhaps our incipient hope that sin is not too serious and does not really separate us from God. Whatever our preconception, the biblical message is clear; we all must take the step for ourselves and receive "the gift of God."

In the final analysis, "the Lord knows those who are his." Our judgment of others on the basis of their words or their external habits may be faulty.

The "universal fatherhood of God" is a widespread view that appeals to many at first. If there was no breach between God and man the death of Christ would have been unnecessary. It's easier to assume that all men are God's children, therefore efforts to "convert" others are in bad taste. Though we all *are* God's offspring by creation (Acts 17:28), we are *not* all God's children spiritually. He is God, the Designer, and desires that all peoples would "*seek* Him and perhaps *reach* out for Him and *find* Him"(Acts 17:27, italics added).

The cross is God's gift; "to all who received him, to those who believed in his name, he gave the right *to become* children of God" (John 1:12, italics added). We believe, receive, and then we *become children of God.* We cannot *become* what we already *are!* Good *news* rather than good *advice* describes the death of Christ most simply: "But God demonstrates his own love for us in this: While we were still sinners, Christ died for us" (Rom. 5:8).

Christ's sacrifice is a pardon and reprieve from death for each of us who is undeserving. There is nothing we must or can do in order to be rescued from alienation from God. We can simply receive Him and His forgiveness as a free gift and so experience eternal life.

"Assurance of Salvation"

The certainty we are forgiven, "assurance of salvation," rests entirely on the substitutionary death of Christ as its base of a restored relationship with the Creator. This assurance is not arrogant presumption that claims, "I am better than you." Rather it is confidence in the trustworthiness of God's Word, the truthfulness of His message to us. God cannot lie. From the cross, just before He died, Jesus said, "It is finished" (John 19:30). So we speak of the "finished work of Christ," expressing our faith that our Lord has already done everything necessary for our salvation.

Becoming a child of God is the beginning, as Jesus called it—*the new birth, new life.* Then we begin to grow spiritually. We will still sin, need daily cleansing, and grow through instructions from our Lord. He will continue to forgive and cleanse us from unrighteous patterns. We are and always will be His children, not alienated and apart from Him. We are assured of our salvation, we belong to Him: "I write these things to you who believe in the name of the Son of God so that you may *know* that you have eternal life" (1 John 5:13, italics added).

Assurance of salvation need not lead us to indifference and smug contentment. It should lead to deep joy and a loving response to Christ as we continue to trust in Him. We are continually reminded, "You are not your own; you were bought at a price. Therefore honor God with your body" (1 Cor. 6:19-20). It's a new life we receive, one that changes our attitudes, motives, values, and will. In ourselves we are incapable of such changes; in Christ, we become new creations (2 Cor. 5:17). It is for this reason that Paul was so adamant in maintaining that the church add nothing to simple trust as a requirement for salvation, and add nothing afterward by way of legal regulation to maintain salvation.

The Gospel is not Christ "plus" something, as good as that something may be. It is Christ *alone.* What matters is His atoning death for us.

God's Love in Action

We live in a world that is acutely aware of man's pain, suffering, and misery. No one is interested in a God who is aloof and untouched by human need, or even in a God who might save sinners from a distance.

The reconciling cross of Christ demonstrates God's desire to be involved in our world. God, in Christ, became involved in this life. He assumed its burdens and entered into its tragedies. Finally, Christ took on full responsibility for this life by becoming "sin for us, so that in him we might become the righteousness of God" (2 Cor. 5:21).

Now we *know* that God is not indifferent to man's tragedy and suffering. In the cross of Christ the affirmation "God is love" takes concrete expression. This is a demonstration of love in action, not only in words. John says, "This is how we know what love is: Jesus Christ laid down his life for us" (1 John 3:16).

Christ's death, in its objective accomplishment and subjective impact, is the central fact of history.

> *Love so amazing, so divine*
> *Demands my soul, my life, my all.*[9]

Man and Sin

W hat is man?" asked the Psalmist David centuries ago. It is striking that this is also the burning question at the dawn of the twenty-first century and the expanding Space Age. Are we merely glorified animals? Are we only the sum total of all our chemicals and their reactions? Or are we more than this?

As scientists decipher the genetic code and begin to unravel the electronic aspects of the brain's functions, the problem of the human identity becomes increasingly urgent. Now we are challenged by the cloning of human genes.

"Who am I?" The question of our identity underlies all we do and all we become. Does it matter what course our lives take? If all we are is a piece of protoplasm, evolved by a mere chance collision of random atoms or cloned in a petri dish, it wouldn't matter who we are. In fact, our answer to the question of identity has enormous influence upon our view of ourselves, our choices, and our goals. Never was it more important for a Christian to understand what the Bible says about mankind. Its truth contains God's anchor in the sea of human speculation.

The Origin of Humanity

The first question to be answered is that of origin. Where did man and woman come from? The first chapter of the Bible brings the pivotal answer: "In the beginning God created the heavens and the earth" (Gen. 1:1). "God said, 'Let us make man *in our image, in our likeness,* and let them rule over the fish of the sea and the birds of the air, over the livestock, over all the earth, and over all the creatures that move along the ground.' So God created man in his own image, in the image of God he created him; male and female he created them" (vv. 26-27, italics added).

Blind chance is nowhere taught in the Scripture for either the creation of the universe or the creation of the human race. We are, specifically, the result of careful and purposeful deliberation by the members of the Triune Godhead.

Adam, the first man, was created in God's own image. John Stott sums it up: "Our chief claim to nobility as human beings is that we were made in the image of God."[1] God's image carries with it the privilege of knowing Him one-on-one and viewing ourselves through His eyes. The first man was called *Adam.* The Hebrew word from which this name comes also carries the connotation of "mankind." It is frequently so used in the Old Testament. God said, "It is not good for the man to be alone" and to complement man, He made a woman to be Adam's helper (Gen. 2:18, 22).

"By faith we understand that the universe was formed at God's command, so that what is seen was not made out of what was visible" (Heb. 11:3). In other words, God created matter *ex nihilo* (out of nothing). He then formed matter into living objects—plants, animals, and human kind. The Bible does not claim to tell us *how* the human race and the universe were created. It does, however, assert emphatically and unambiguously *that God brought all there is into being.*

Nowhere does the Bible attempt to *prove* God. It *assumes* Him. Without apology the Bible begins with the assumption that God exists and existed eternally before creating life on earth. It supports this belief with the evidence of the life, death, and resurrection of Christ. Such an assumption is not naive or unintellectual, but rather rests on the strong, rational evidence presented in chapter 2.

It helps to keep in mind that those who reject the biblical view of Creation also begin with presuppositions and assumptions on which they base *their* claims. *Everyone* begins with some kind of an assumption or a bias not totally provable in the purely scientific sense. The key question we must all ask is: "On what evidence do our assumptions rest?"

Adam and Eve Were Uniquely Created

Both Old Testament and New Testament writers viewed Adam as a person, a person as historical as Jesus Christ Himself. Jesus spoke of the creation of man, confirming the Genesis account (Matt. 19:4). The Apostle Paul also considered Adam to be a distinct individual as well as the prototype, the norm, of sin-bent man (Rom. 5:12-21; 1 Cor. 15:22). These accounts leave no room for mythical or allegorical interpretations of the historicity of Adam's creation and subsequent fall.

Adam was distinct and unique from the rest of creation. He was to subdue it and have dominion over it. He was at the top of all living beings. He was a separate individual. He asked questions, had a sense of right and wrong (he hid himself after he sinned), and had the power of choice. In three areas man was set apart from all other creatures:

- self-consciousness,

- capacity for intelligent reasoning, and

- moral and spiritual sense.

Look at your pet dog. Has that dog ever asked, "Is there a God?" It has been said that no creature other than man has ever been observed building a cathedral.

Body, Soul, and Spirit

Genesis 2 gives further information on the creation of man: "The Lord God formed the man from the dust of the ground and breathed into his nostrils the breath of life, and the man became a living being" (v. 7). Here we see two elements involved in man's creation. One is "the dust of the ground." The other is "the

> **Nowhere does the Bible attempt to prove God. It assumes Him.**
>
> **Man is a unique creation. Has your pet dog ever asked: "Is there a God?"**

breath of life," that is, God's breath. The union of these *two* elements made man a living being.

Man is unquestionably more than just a body. But are the components of his being *three* (body, soul, and spirit) or *two* (body and soul)? The Old Testament does not have a fixed term for this immaterial part of man's nature. The terms *soul, heart,* and *spirit* are used as counterparts to the material side. With the term *body,* they define the whole man. David wrote in a prayer, "My *soul* thirsts for you, my *body* longs for you" (Ps. 63:1, italics added). Other verses speak just as plainly of *three* aspects of man's being: " My *soul* yearns, even faints, for the courts of the Lord; my *heart* and my *flesh* cry out for the living God" (Ps. 84:2, italics added).

Heart in the Old Testament is referred to 29 times as the physical organ. But there are 822 additional references referring to personality, emotions, intellect, and volition. These references describe the inner person, the nonphysical part of the real you.[2]

Should the God-breathed part of man be viewed as two parts—i.e., soul and spirit separately—or as one? Hammond observes:

> "Soul" and "spirit" are certainly not to be regarded as synonymous in scriptural language. But on the other hand, they are not kept invariably distinct. . . . It would seem best to regard them as *differing aspects* of the *same* essence . . .but there is a substratum which is common to both soul and spirit.[3]

The Bible always views each person as a unity, both material and immaterial. The Resurrection shows that each of us is as essentially body as well as soul and spirit. Most of us know our essential self is more than our bodies. The notion that man is a soul imprisoned in a body is a Greek concept, not a biblical one.

What Is God's Image?

What does it mean that man was created in the image and likeness of God? This statement certainly does not imply any *physical* likeness to God. Scripture teaches that God is a spirit and does not have physical parts like a man (John 4:24). The Bible uses anthropomorphic expressions, such as "the hand of God" only to accommodate our human incapacity to think in any other terms. The strong prohibition against man's representing God by graven images was given because no one had ever seen God; therefore, no one could know what He looks like. Nothing on earth *could* represent His Spirit (Deut. 4:15-23).

The image of God in man has to do, rather, with *personality*. According to D.M. Edwards, "Man has a free, self-conscious, rational personality like that of God, a nature capable of distinguishing right and wrong, of choosing the right and rejecting wrong, and of ascending to the heights of spiritual attainment and communion with God."[4]

The human qualities of feeling, caring, communicating come from God. Even joy, sorrow, and desiring relationship are part of His personality.

• The original man was *intelligent*. He could give names to all the animals when they were presented to him (Gen. 2:19-20). He had the power of reasoning and thought. In speaking, he could connect words and ideas. He could and did commune with God.

• *Moral and spiritual* qualities differentiated mankind from all other creatures. God's image gave them an awareness, a sense of *right and wrong* (Gen. 3). This "knowing" from God means that God's people love love and hate evil and differentiate between the two options. This is not optional software! The New Testament calls this "conscience" (1 Tim. 1:5).

• *Individual separateness* distinguishes God and mankind from each other—each being their own person. All people are endowed with God's image and separate from all other people. Obviously, I am not you and you are not me. And neither of us is God.

The significance of this separateness is that it clarifies our understanding of God as an approachable individual. He is not an amorphous blob, a genie, a ghost, or even "The Force." We can communicate person-to-person and understand each other.

The Choice

Originally, man was holy and the basic inclination of his nature was toward God. He was not *neutral* toward God. The creation of the "new man in Christ" is based on the pattern of the original creation of man.

At Creation, man had no original inward tendency to sin, as we now have. Though he was capable of being tempted, he was neither *compelled* nor *impelled* to sin. Both Adam and Eve deliberately *chose* to sin, as a free act. In the words of a famous phrase: "Man did not have inability to sin; he had ability not to sin. He could choose."

Had things remained as they were in the original Creation, all would have been well. Sin and death, with all their disastrous consequences for the human race, would never have come into being if Adam and Eve had chosen to obey rather than disobey by asserting their wills against God. But they *did* assert themselves against God, and their rebellion brought titanic disaster to all their descendants.

It is significant and intensely interesting that most, if not all, primitive religious traditions have, in one form or another, a belief in such a cataclysmic event, a falling down, so to speak. "The Fall," as it is called, permanently altered what previously was an idyllic relationship between God and man. Even in primitive animistic societies, which worship many gods, there is belief in a high-sky God, an unreachable Creator. Such cultures hold that after the passing of the golden age of intimate contact, this God becomes aloof from man, unreachable. Typically, the high-sky God, as they see it, now deals with human beings only through the lesser gods. All of these ideas seem to be echoes and reflections—distorted, faint, or mutilated by the passage of time—of the event clearly described in the Bible (Gen. 3).

Not Talking Robots

The sin of Adam and Eve, as we have seen, was something for which they were personally responsible. They did not have sinful natures such as we have, so the temptation to sin must have come from outside them. The Bible describes this source as "the serpent" (Gen. 3:1), used by the Devil to alienate man from God. The serpent thus remains a symbol of deceit and is identified with Satan in Revelation 12:9.

Why did God not prevent evil from entering the universe since He knew in advance what would happen? Why did He not make man incapable of sinning? God *could* have prevented evil from entering our world, but had He done so, we would not have the image of God or be human beings with freedom of

> God did not want talking dolls or robots. He created humankind with the ability to choose.

choice. We would be robots, or "talking dolls" that always speak the same words when someone pulls the string.

Though we have no final answers to sin's origin, God knew what would happen and, "thought it was worth the risk," as C.S. Lewis explained. It is useless to speculate endlessly about the *origin* of evil. Each of us, however, faces the *fact* of evil, and the whole of God's redemptive program has to do with combating it.

God is not the author of sin. Had our first parents not disobeyed Him, sin would never have entered the human race. Several facets of man's first sin are clear, described in Genesis 3.

- Adam and Eve were first tempted to *doubt* God's Word. ("Did God really say that?")

- The serpent led them to *disbelieve* God. ("You will not surely die.")

- They *believed the serpent* and gave in to the temptation.

- They *disobeyed* God's command and ate the forbidden fruit.

The results of man's disobedience were immediate and obvious—separation from God and awareness of guilt. The consequences which God had warned them of involved both physical and spiritual death, that is, separation from their Maker. Hard physical labor and sorrow followed for all mankind. Man's fall involved the whole natural creation as well (Rom. 8:21-22). Summarized, the results were

- the image of God in man was badly marred in both its moral and its natural dimensions;

- man lost his original inclination toward God;

- man's desires inclined away from his Creator; and

- man's intellect became bound, his emotions corrupted, and his will enslaved.

Total Depravity

Some skeptics today speak about man as "evolving" from a primitive condition, but the Bible (Rom. 1:18-32) sadly portrays his *descent* rather than *ascent*. The result has been given the theological term "total depravity." This expression of man's condition after the Fall has been widely misunderstood, with the result that the Christian position regarding man's sinful nature has sometimes been unjustly caricatured. Simply stated the doctrine of depravity

> was never intended to convey the meaning that man is as bad as he possibly can be and that every trace of moral rectitude has been lost in fallen man. "Total depravity" is intended to indicate that the evil principle . . . has invaded each part of human nature, that there is no part of it which can now invariably perform righteous acts or invariably think righteous thoughts.[5]

Man's total depravity affects *every area of his life*—he is blighted, but not everything about him is *totally bad*. His depravity is total in that without God's grace he would be forever lost and apart from God.

The tragedy of the Fall went far beyond Adam and Eve. It was racewide in its effect: "Therefore, just as sin entered the world through one man, and death through sin, and in this way death came to all men, because all sinned" (Rom. 5:12).

Theologians have generally held three appraisals of the effect of the Fall on the human race.

1. The British monk Pelagius concluded that Adam's sin *did not directly affect other men* in any way. He said that all men could be sinless if they chose. Pelagius therefore reasoned that since a man can live free from sin, he must have been born into the world free from sin. Consequently, Adam's sin must have affected only Adam, thus denying "original sin." From there, he asserted that man has *no need of supernatural help* to live a righteous life. Pelagius did, however, recognize the force of sin's habit and its harmful example to others.

2. Augustine, the great bishop of North Africa, believed that *Adam's guilt and corruption passed to all men*. He rose to do battle with Pelagius' heretical view. Augustine insisted that Adam transmitted to his posterity both his guilt and the corruption belonging to it because of the unity of the human race. The nature that man now has, said Augustine, is like the corrupted nature of Adam. Man has lost his freedom not to sin. Augustine coined the phrase "The will is free, but not freed." Though he has a free choice, man *chooses* a perverse course.

3. Some theologians believed a semi-Pelagianism theory, stating: *Man lost only his special gift of righteousness.* He is only *half* sick. Roman Catholics generally hold this halfway position. In the Fall man lost the supernatural gift of righteousness which was not his by nature anyway, but had been added by God. Man, according to this view, still has a special gift of the Spirit which is sufficient to enable him to be righteous if he allows his will to cooperate with God's Spirit.

Augustine's Appraisal

The Augustinian view is closest to the biblical view—that man inherits a tendency to sin that always, to some extent, makes itself manifest. "The Lord saw how great man's wickedness on the earth had become, and that every inclination of the thoughts of his heart was only evil all the time" (Gen. 6:5). When David said, "Surely I was sinful at birth, sinful from the time my mother conceived me" (Ps. 51:5), he was not speaking of the act of conception as sinful, but of the inherited bias to sin.

The Scripture makes plain, there may be a difference between men in their *degree* of sin, but there is no difference in the *fact* of sin (Rom. 3:9-10, 22-23; Isa. 53:6). The whole world is under judgment (Rom. 3:19), and all men are apart from Christ, rebels against God, and held accountable to God. They are therefore deserving of His wrath (Eph. 2:2-4).

The universality of sin has been recorded since the beginning of time. Anyone who has ever had children recognizes clearly that self-centeredness shows up in the next generation at a very early age. You don't have to teach a child to be selfish. Parents spend much effort to overcome this tendency in their children, but the only one who has ever escaped this inherited bias toward sin is the Lord Jesus Himself.

Adam's Legacy

The Bible pictures Adam as our "representative" when he sinned. Just as when our government declares war, it represents, affects, and involves us,

Adam represents the rest of the human race (Rom. 5:12-19). We tend to think that things might have turned out differently if we had been in Adam's place. But as history has recounted, each of us has done as Adam did, ratifying the decision of our forebears, and disobeying God's commands. Can any of us claim we have never sinned? And so we are justly condemned today not only for Adam's sin, but for our own sins.

Sin, for all of us, does not begin with overt acts, nor is it limited to them. Our acts proceed from a corrupt heart and mind, deep inside. They begin, as the poet said, as "a cuticle of dust, a cobweb on the soul," barely recognized at first. In other words, *we are not sinners because we sin—we sin because we are sinners.* An apple tree is not an apple tree because it bears apples; it bears apples because it has the nature of an apple tree. Sins are the acts (or the apples); sin is our corrupt nature (the apple tree). "This is the verdict: Light has come into the world, but men loved darkness instead of light because their deeds were evil" (John 3:19).

Jesus Christ Our "Representative"

The *Good News* is that believers are represented in Christ! As in Adam all die, so in Christ all believers will be made alive (Rom. 5:19). The glory of the Gospel is that God did something for us in Christ that we could not do for ourselves. Through Christ, the second Adam, we are given a *new nature*. We are turned to forgiveness and righteousness. To accomplish in us this new nature, spiritual life, God provided the "Lamb of God," a full sacrifice, to take away the sins of world. The solution was radical but demonstrates the determined love and grace of God: "For the grace of God that brings salvation has appeared to all men. It teaches us to say 'No' to ungodliness" (Titus 2:11-12).

Realistically, Scripture emphasizes man's ability to reject sin and receive Christ. But *each person* must make the choice.

Seeing with God's Eyes

Still the question comes, how can we be responsible for being sinners if God gave us a hopeless start in life? How can He then condemn us? The answer comes repeatedly that He enables us to close the gap and escape judgment.

All people are not equally bad, and God knows this very well. The verse "all have sinned" (Rom. 3:23) does not imply that all are as bad as they might be. But in relation to God, the holy, sovereign God, we all come short. He is our measuring rod. You probably know honest, kind, and upright people who are not to be compared with vicious predators or intentional cheats. Humanly, there are great differences.

> **God's holiness is 100 percent perfect. God's love for mankind is 100 percent perfect.**

To see with God's eyes, suppose we were to compare one person's morals to being in Death Valley, 280 feet below sea level; another person's morals to being in Denver, the mile-high city; and another person's morals to the peak of Mount Everest, altitude 29,000 feet. The person in Death Valley represents the most ruthless lowlife in society. The person in Denver is the "average man," and the one on Mount Everest is the best person you can imagine. The enormous differences in their altitude, or elevation, are apparent. By comparison, God's standard of holiness (100 percent perfect) is represented by the earth's distance to the moon. Morally and without His help, we are far from God's holiness. In recent decades, we have had an opportunity to see how Mount Everest, Denver, and Death Valley look from the moon. They are all the same!

From our human standpoint, there are great differences in men's sinfulness, but—contrasted with the infinite holiness of God, the moon, all men are equally lost, estranged from their Creator.

No "Big Sins or Little Sins"

It is easy for us to shun a discussion of sin and treat it rather lightly. "Big sins and little sins" we call them. Sin is more than mere self-centeredness. Only God's view can give us the true perspective. He is our perfect God. A few factors can clarify the meaning of sin.

• All sin is primarily directed *against* God. He is the One who designed us and gave us the rule book! The Old Testament King David, though he had wronged Bathsheba in adultery and had murdered Uriah, cried out to the Lord. "Against you, *you only*, have I sinned and done what is evil in your sight" (Ps. 51:4, italics added). He saw God's view of his actions.

• The first sin of Adam and Eve was the prototype, the precedent, the model, of all other sins. It *broke God's commandment*, as does all sin. The commandment "don't eat from that one tree" showed God's authority, goodness, wisdom, justice, faithfulness and grace. In their transgression, Adam and Eve rejected God's authority, doubted His goodness, disputed His wisdom, repudiated His justice, contradicted His truthfulness, and spurned His grace.

Sin's two aspects are an active, overt "breaking the law" (1 John 3:4) and a passive *failure to do good* (James 4:17). These we call sins of *commission* and sins of *omission*. *The Book of Common Prayer* adequately summarizes it: "We have done those things we ought not to have done and we have left undone those things we ought to have done."

Sin, regardless of the type, will always *bring disastrous consequences*. Sin is the opposite of God's perfection.[6] It brought disastrous consequences to Adam, to humanity, and to society in general. We think no one will know, we can get away with it. We want to make our own rules. We know better!

The Grandeur of the Grace of God

If no power were strong enough to change human nature, there would be no hope for man. But the good news of the Gospel is that there *is* such power—in Christ: "Where sin increased, grace increased all the more" (Rom. 5:20).

An understanding of what the Bible teaches about the nature of man in Creation along with the devastating effects of the Fall helps us comprehend the grandeur of the grace of God. Any skepticism about the truth of God's grace stems from an *inflated* view of man or a *shrunken* view of God and His holiness.

The new man "created in Christ Jesus" is *renewed* or remade in the image of God in righteousness. The former pattern of ignoring God's will is changed. "Put off your old self . . . to be made new in the attitude of your minds; and to put on the new self, created to be like God in true righteousness and holiness" (Eph. 4:22-24). "You . . . have put on the new self, which is being renewed in

> Christ puts a new man in a suit—not just a new suit on a man. Skepticism about God's grace stems either from an inflated view of man or a shrunken view of God.

knowledge in the image of its Creator" (Col 3:9-10).

Through Christ we are not only forgiven our individual acts of sin, but we receive a new nature. The Gospel solution is radical, not merely one of outward reform, but inward reform, transforming the heart, the emotions, the will. Someone has said, "Christ puts a new man in the suit—not just a new suit on the man." When a person is changed by Christ, his clothing (his attitudes) will change as well. God has made full provision, through the sacrifice of Christ, for us to escape judgment and have a new life.

These issues are matters of life and death between us and our Maker. Man does not live and die like an animal. Death does not end our existence. The soul and spirit survive the body. Jesus Himself spoke clearly of this continued existence for both the saved and the lost: "I am the resurrection and the life. He who believes in me will live, even though he dies; and whoever lives and believes in me will never die" (John 11:25-26).

In the story of the rich man and Lazarus (Luke 16:19-31), Christ taught the continued conscious existence of the unjust. The whole teaching of the New Testament about future judgment rests on the assumption that the soul survives after death: "Man is destined to die once, and after that to face judgment" (Heb. 9:27; see also Rom. 2:5-11; 2 Cor. 5:10).

The Resurrection applies not only to those who will be raised to be with Christ forever (1 Thess. 4:16), but also to the wicked, who will be raised for judgment. Jesus declared: "A time is coming when all who are in their graves will hear his voice and come out—those who have done good will rise to live, and those who have done evil will rise to be condemned" (John 5:28-29).

The sobering truth that we exist forever makes it imperative that we give thought to our nature, condition, and destiny while we are still able to do what is needful.

In answer to the question "Who am I?" the Bible teaches that each of us is a personality created purposefully by God in His own image. It teaches that we have eternal significance in God's eyes and our souls are worth more than the whole world (Mark 8:36).

God Himself has provided a plan and a purpose, which He holds out to each one of us. The choice is ours as morally responsible individuals to respond to Him. He literally yearns for us to respond in faith and to live in His presence forever rather than in everlasting separation from Him.

The Holy Spirit

Of the three persons in the Godhead—Father, Son, and Holy Spirit—the Holy Spirit is doubtless the least known and understood. Yet He is most vitally and intimately involved in our initial conversion and birth into the family of God and in our ongoing development as Christians. Our awareness of His work in our lives as Christians can ripen into a relationship with Him that brings us power, joy, and hope.

Of primary importance is this truth: the Holy Spirit is as much a person as God the Father and God the Son. He is not an impersonal "it," nor an influence, a phantom, or an apparition.

Our view of the Holy Spirit may be colored by our use of the term *spirit* in casual conversation. We speak of the "spirit of the times" or say that "a spirit of expectancy swept the crowd as it awaited the arrival of a celebrity."

Some of the biblical metaphors referring to the Holy Spirit may reinforce the idea that He is not a personal being. Both the Hebrew and Greek words translated *spirit* mean basically "breath" or "wind" or "spirit" in the sense of the vitality of living creatures (Gen. 6:17). In Greek, the word is in the neuter gender. The context of various passages, however, has brought careful translators to use "*the Spirit himself*" (Rom. 8:16, 26). Even the *New King James Version* and other versions read, "the Spirit himself." Also, Jesus never referred to the Holy Spirit as "it" (John 14:15-17).

> **The perfection of the Godhead is seen in the work of the Holy Spirit communicating everywhere. He speaks in the United States, Jakarta, and to all peoples.**

Misunderstanding may also partially stem from the fact that the work of the Holy Spirit is not as visibly prominent as that of the Father and of the Son. Jesus, in speaking of the gift of the Spirit said, "He will not speak on his own; he will speak only what he hears, and he will tell you what is yet to come" (John 16:13).

The perfection and character of the Godhead can be seen in the work of the Holy Spirit extending to the entire world—from Jakarta to the United States. God is everywhere in our world through the work of the Holy Spirit, who speaks to "every tribe and every nation," even to you and me.

Then too the symbols used in Scripture to describe the influence of the Spirit include oil, fire, and water—all of which are impersonal. However, thoughtful reading of the Scriptures shows the Father and the Son are described in similar figurative ways—as light, bread of life, living water, etc.

Personality—Mind, Feelings, Will

• When we speak of the *personality of the Holy Spirit,* the term has double significance. *God was not made in the image of man, but man in the image of God.* The word *personality* is not a perfect term, but for both the Spirit and God it is descriptive of their nature. It is comforting to know that the Holy Spirit has a mind, feelings, and a will. He can think, has emotions, and can choose just as God the Father and God the Son do.

Jesus gave some of the clearest scriptural teaching about the Holy Spirit in John chapters 14–17. He called the Spirit the Comforter (KJV), or Counselor (NIV). "The Counselor, the Holy Spirit, whom the Father will send in my name, will teach you all things and will remind you of everything I have said to you" (John 14:26).

The terms *Comforter* or *Counselor* convey the idea of One who acts as our attorney and on whom a believer calls for help. Obviously, counseling and comforting would not be possible if the Spirit were merely an impersonal influence.

In John 16:7, as in the previous reference, the emphasis is on when Christ will leave the disciples and go back to the Father. Jesus promised that the Father would send the Holy Spirit to represent the Lord Jesus Himself. This change, Jesus said, would be beneficial for His disciples. Again, an impersonal force could hardly improve on the personal presence of Jesus Christ.

• The Holy Spirit is *equal* in His personal nature to the Father and the Son. We cannot explain many biblical references to the Holy Spirit apart from this understanding. The Holy Spirit living within the Christian is described as "God's Spirit lives in you" (1 Cor. 3:16).

The story of Ananias further illustrates this equality. Ananias was struck dead because he "lied to the Holy Spirit" (Acts 5:3). The Spirit may be *grieved* (Eph. 4:30) and *sinned against* by unforgivable blasphemy (Mark 3:29). Sin against God is equally sin against the Son and the Holy Spirit. He is equal in His personal nature to the Father and the Son. The Trinity, although not easy to understand, is *"three* in One."

• The Holy Spirit *does things, acts,* as only a person would. He *speaks:* "The Spirit told Philip, 'Go to that chariot and stay near it' " (Acts 8:29). He *strives:* "My Spirit will not contend with man forever" (Gen. 6:3). He *helps:* "The Spirit helps us in our weaknesses . . . the Spirit himself intercedes for us (Rom. 8:26). He *reveals, searches, and knows:* "God has revealed it to us by his Spirit. The Spirit searches all things, even the deep things of God. . . . No one knows the thoughts of God except the Spirit of God" (1 Cor. 2:10-11).

• Finally, the Holy Spirit distributes *spiritual gifts* "to each one, just as he [the Spirit] determines" (1 Cor. 12:11). None of these verbs could rightly be used of a mere influence.

The Holy Spirit Is Deity

The Holy Spirit is not only a person—He is Deity. The Apostle Paul said, "Now the Lord is the Spirit" (2 Cor. 3:17). And again, "Don't you know that you yourselves are God's temple and that God's Spirit lives in you?" (1 Cor. 3:16) At the gathering of the Council of Jerusalem the disciples declared, "It seemed good to the Holy Spirit and to us . . ." (Acts 15:28).

Jesus said that blasphemy against the Holy Spirit is worse than blasphemy against the Son of Man. The implication is that blasphemy against the Spirit maligns and discredits God (Matt. 12:31).

The Holy Spirit possesses attributes that belong only to Deity. He is *eternal:* "Christ, who through the eternal Spirit offered himself" (Heb. 9:14). He is *omnipresent:* "Where can I go from your Spirit? Where can I flee from your presence?" (Ps. 139:7) He is the "Spirit of *life*" (Rom. 8:2) and the "Spirit of *truth*" (John 16:13). This list of the Holy Spirit's work certainly speaks of the divine power of God, embodied in Him when He comes and dwells within the Christian.

The Holy Spirit in the Old Testament

Five differing aspects are discernible of the work of the Spirit in the Old Testament.[1]

1. The work of the Spirit helped *create the universe and man* (Gen. 1:2): "The Spirit of God was hovering over the waters." Job said, "The Spirit of God has made me; the breath of the Almighty gives me life" (33:4).

2. The work of the Spirit *equipped individuals for service.* He conferred power on judges and warriors. For instance, "The Spirit of the Lord came upon [Samson] in power" (Jud. 14:6). The Israelites cried out to God, and He gave them Othniel, "and the Spirit of the Lord came upon him, so that he became Israel's judge and went to war" (Jud. 3:10). The Spirit came upon people for a particular purpose in this manner, but did not necessarily transform their moral character unless they called out for it.

He also gave wisdom and skill for particular jobs, including those of a nonspiritual nature, to various individuals. Bezaleel was filled with the Spirit to work in gold, silver, and bronze for the tabernacle (Ex. 31:2-5).

3. The work of the Spirit *inspired the prophets.* Usually they began their message with "This is what the Lord says." At times, however, they also attributed their message to the Holy Spirit: "The Spirit came into me and raised me to my feet, and I heard him speaking to me" (Ezek. 2:2). And Moses exclaimed, "Are you jealous for my sake? I wish that all the Lord's people were prophets and that the Lord would put His Spirit on them!" (Num. 11:29)

Isaiah said, "I heard the voice of the Lord" (Isa. 6:8). Later, the Apostle Paul said, "The Holy Spirit spoke the truth to your forefathers when He said through Isaiah the prophet: . . . 'You will be ever hearing but never understanding'" (Acts 28:25-26).

4. The work of the Holy Spirit *produced moral living.* David, in the agony of repentance for his dual sin of adultery and murder, pleaded for God to create in him a clean heart. He also begged, "Do not . . . take your Holy Spirit from me" (Ps. 51:11). The Spirit, David knew, is good, and He leads men to do God's will (Ps. 143:10; 139:23-24).

5. The work of the Spirit *foretold the coming of the Messiah.* The references that anticipate Christ are of two kinds. There were those that prophesied a direct indwelling of the Spirit in one messianic figure. Other prophecies contained a more general message, telling about the new covenant people of God, with the Spirit being given to all people of all classes. (See Isa. 9:2-7; 42:1-4.)

Scripture suggests the Holy Spirit caused men to grow more and more conscious of their inner need for God's help if they were to serve the Lord and be morally pure. In the latter parts of the Old Testament, some scholars detect an awareness, on the part of believers, that the human government of Israel would never succeed in achieving the purposes of Jehovah, and that, in time, the Spirit would be given to all God's people, not only to the people of Israel.[2]

Holy Spirit Came On Temporarily

In the Old Testament the Spirit came *on individuals temporarily,* generally for a particular task and for a period of time. Then, when the occasion for His coming was over, He withdrew. While men could have an intimate relationship with Him, as shown by David's experience, the fellowship was not as personal or as permanent as is possible since Pentecost. For instance, Samson's tragic downfall resulted from his turning away from the Lord and the Spirit withdrew. He had become so insensitive to the Lord that he was not even aware that the Spirit had left him (Jud. 16:20).

Throughout its pages the writers of the Old Testament expressed a longing for help, God's power, and an ultimate relationship with Him. The psalmists and the prophets poured out their hearts over and over and God responded unerringly. God's interventions were attributed to the Spirit of the Lord, God's Spirit, the Spirit of God, or simply the Spirit. Only three times is "Holy Spirit" used in the Old Testament (Ps. 51:11; Isa. 63:10ff). The New Testament uses "Holy Spirit" over 250 times when referring to God's Spirit.[3] Thus, the Old Testament period could not be called "the age of the Spirit" as our age is called.

Just as the truth of the Trinity is hinted at in the Old Testament but awaits its fullest expression in the New, so with truth about the Holy Spirit. His personality and deity are evident in the Old Testament, but the full expression of His activity is given only in the New Testament. The New Testament completes the picture.

The Old Testament Foretold His Pouring Out on All People

The Spirit's work in the Old Testament was *foretelling the sublime fulfillment of God's covenant* promised to Israel and poured out on "all people." This was confirmed and reaffirmed through the words of many of the prophets, who predicted hope and optimism for the future. "I will pour out my Spirit on your offspring, and my blessing on your descendants" (Isa. 44:3). "I will give you a new heart and put a new spirit in you" (Ezek. 36:26; see also v. 27). "I will pour out my Spirit on all people. Your sons and your daughters will prophesy, your old men will dream dreams, your young men will see visions. Even on my servants, both men and women, I will pour out my Spirit in those days" (Joel 2:28-29).

These promises and other similar ones kept hopes high for a day of complete deliverance and peace. They embraced all people from every strata of society, not just a select few. The expression of a "pouring out" was enough to make people dream dreams as never before.

This extraordinary foretelling was always joined with the prophecies of the long-anticipated Messiah, the Redeemer, one messianic figure. John the Baptist saw Jesus and proclaimed to the people, "I have baptized you with water; but he will baptize you with the Holy Spirit." Shortly thereafter at His baptism, Jesus came out of the water and the Spirit descended on Him "like a dove" (Mark 1:10). In His own words, Jesus said that "streams of living water" will flow from those who believe in Him. Then John explained, "By this [statement] he meant the Spirit, whom those who believed in him were later to receive" (John 7:38-39). Succeeding events confirmed that "the Spirit of the Sovereign Lord was on him," the Messiah, the Christ (Isa. 61:1).

Jesus identified Himself with the promises of a Redeemer early in His ministry. In His hometown synagogue in Nazareth He stood up to read. A special attendant handed Him a scroll of the Prophet Isaiah. He unrolled the scroll and began to read the 800-year-old document. He chose the words: "The Spirit of the Sovereign Lord is on me, because the Lord has anointed me to preach good news to the poor" (Isa. 61:1). After handing the scroll back to the attendant, He sat down and made this unprecedented announcement: "Today this scripture is fulfilled in your hearing" (Luke 4:21).

Arrival of the Promised Gift

The gift of the Holy Spirit was increasingly unfolded in Jesus' lifetime on earth. He had a particularly intimate relationship with the Holy Spirit. He was *conceived* by the Holy Spirit and *born* of Him (Luke 1:35). Jesus was *led* by the Spirit (Matt. 4:1). He was *anointed* for His ministry by the Spirit in a special way at His baptism (Matt. 3:13-17). He *offered* Himself as a sacrifice through the Spirit (Heb. 9:14), and He was *raised* from the dead by the power of the Spirit (Rom. 1:4). He gave *commandments* to the apostles, and through them to the church, by the Spirit (Acts 1:2).

Finally, following His death and resurrection, Jesus gave His disciples His last instructions: "Wait for the gift my Father promised. . . . You will be baptized with the Holy Spirit" (Acts 1:4-5).

Fifty days after the Sabbath of the Passover Week He had celebrated with them, the "Gift" came. This feast, called "Pentecost," meaning fifty, was the day of the Jewish Feast of Harvest to give thanks for the grain harvest (Ex. 23:15-16).

While approximately 120 were gathered in Jerusalem for prayer, suddenly a violent wind came from heaven as did tongues of fire. Then "all of them were filled with the Holy Spirit and began to speak in other tongues as the Spirit enabled them" (Acts 2:1-4). As the noise attracted a crowd, Peter stood before them and with raised voice told them: "This

is what was spoken by the prophet Joel." Then word for word, he recited
Joel 2:28-32. His entire message described the life, death, resurrection,
miracles, and promises of Jesus Christ, ending this way: "God has made
this Jesus, whom you crucified, both Lord and Christ" (Acts 2:36).

Only two other incidents are recorded of the Holy Spirit's coming on
a group in such power. The first is Peter speaking to the Gentiles in
Caesarea (Acts 10:34). The second incident is when Paul was on a missionary journey. He found that the Ephesians, although believers, had
not even heard of the Holy Spirit (Acts 19:1-6).

The Work of the Divine Helper

The Holy Spirit has many descriptive titles including "the Spirit of
grace" (Heb. 10:29); the Spirit of truth (1 John 5:6); "the Spirit of wisdom and of understanding, the Spirit of counsel and of power, the Spirit
of knowledge and of the fear of the Lord" (Isa. 11:2). He is the "Spirit of
promise," that is, the One who came in fulfillment of Christ's promise
(Eph. 1:13). He is also called, "the Spirit of glory" (1 Peter 4:14). The
Holy Spirit, then, is completely personal and completely God.

The Holy Spirit is the *executor* of the purposes and plans of the
Godhead. Though the Holy Spirit is self-effacing, His is the direct work
of God and vitally affects each of us as individuals. He is active at various levels. He is the One who carries out God's purposes—creation, conviction, regeneration, enlightenment, sanctification, and glorification.

Jesus' outline of the work of the Spirit so far as humanity is very specific. In John 16:8-11 we read about the convicting role of the Spirit.

• The Holy Spirit convicts of *guilt in regard to sin*. Without the unveiling
of the Holy Spirit, we would not believe we are really sinning. Why
should the sight of a man crucified 2,000 years ago tear at the heart of
people centuries later? This is the work of the Holy Spirit or else we
would not know our need of a Savior.

The Holy Spirit is the One who brings conviction of sin to an individual (John 16:8). Whenever a person comes to a sense of his own sinfulness, whether by the preached, written, or personally spoken word, the
Spirit of God has been at work.

• The Holy Spirit convicts of *righteousness*. The meaning of this is only
clear when we see the righteousness of Jesus Christ, who gave His life for

the world. The sting of sin and the imperative of righteousness for all of us is found in the cross. The Spirit's work is to reveal what the holiness of God desires for us. Through His death He *gives us* His righteousness; He makes us sensitive to any antithesis of God's revealed righteousness.

• The Holy Spirit convicts of *judgment to come*. Only through the work of the Spirit in our lives can we understand the imperative of judgment. Why not let all be forgiven? Why can we not do what we all like, regardless of consequences? The prospect of judgment is certain and brought Jesus Christ to take our judgment upon Himself on the cross. The Spirit convinces us of the deliverance available, and the cross is our exit from disaster and our entrance into deliverance (John 16:8-11).[4]

The result of this conviction by the Holy Spirit is His work of *regeneration*, the new birth: "So it is with everyone born of the Spirit" (John 3:8). He indwells everyone who is in the church of Jesus Christ by the new birth. It is emphatically true that "if anyone does not have the Spirit of Christ, he does not belong to Christ" (Rom. 8:9). Equally true is that *every* Christian has the Holy Spirit with His counseling, help, and conviction, beginning from the time of belief and commitment.

Gives Spiritual Gifts

Paul describes the church as the body of Christ. All believers are joined into one body, stressing its unity, even as the physical body works as one. In this context, the Holy Spirit administers spiritual gifts (the Greek *charismata*) for the good of the whole body: "The manifestation of the Spirit is given for the *common good*" (1 Cor. 12:7, italics added; see also the entire chapter). The body of Christ is the place where the Holy Spirit teaches a new Christian to grow, learn, and serve.

Through the work of the Holy Spirit, "to each one" is given the manifestation of the Spirit. There are differing gifts but the *same* Spirit . . . the *same* Lord . . . the *same* God working in all people (Rom. 12:4, italics added). There are four lists of gifts given in the New Testament, showing some differences and some overlap. Each Christian has at least one gift, others more, but always, gifts are the work of the Holy Spirit in our lives.[5]

Briefly, the list from 1 Corinthians gives a good starting point. *Wisdom* is defined as divine insights that come from the mind of God and His Word. *Knowledge*, from the Greek *gnosis*, is a more practical kind of insight into everyday living. *Faith* might be called a special potency of trust in the truth of God that can "move mountains." *Prophecy* gives the idea of preaching rather than foretelling. Deeds of *healing, distinguishing spirits, tongues,* and *interpretation* are also named.

No doubt there are some differences of interpretation among Christians in the four passages concerning spiritual gifts. We have seen

WHAT DOES THE HOLY SPIRIT DO?

Guides to truth John 16:13

Reveals Jesus John 16:14

Comforts John 14:16

Counsels John 14:26

Gives wisdom Eph. 1:17

Prays for me Rom. 8:27

Gives me power Acts 1:8

Helps my weaknesses Rom. 8:26

Gives spiritual gifts 1 Cor. 12:11

Gives spiritual fruit Gal. 5:22-23

that the Holy Spirit is the Author of the Scriptures, the One who inspired them (2 Peter 1:20-21). He is also the One who interprets them and guides our hearts and minds. He is the Spirit of wisdom and revelation (Eph. 1:17), and He interprets the mind of God for us through these Scriptures (1 Cor. 2:9-14).

Among the gifts, speaking in tongues is doubtless the most controversial, followed by "second baptism of the Spirit" and signs and wonders. First Corinthians 14 gives helpful direction for each of these disputed areas.

It has been rightly observed that this "illuminating" work of the Holy Spirit never becomes so mystical and subjective that *grammatical* and *historical consistency* of the Bible need be abandoned. By misunderstanding the role of the Holy Spirit in interpreting the Scriptures, some have made the Bible almost a magical book, equating their subjective feelings with the authority of the Spirit. The Christ of Scripture will always be central to any true work of the Holy Spirit.

Gives Spiritual Fruit

When the Holy Spirit does His work of producing His fruit in us, we find that "*love, joy, peace, patience, kindness, goodness, faithfulness, gentleness and self-control*" (Gal. 5:22-23, italics added) are ours as we submit to the mind of Christ, the example of His life, and the internal guidance of the Spirit.

Every Christian is indwelt by the Holy Spirit, and He is a constant guide to the individual Christian: "Those who are led by the Spirit of God are sons of God" (Rom. 8:14). We are instructed to "live by the Spirit" (Gal. 5:16). His leadership is one of the signs that an individual is really a child of God: He leads us today as He led and guided the early Christians in the Book of Acts. Peter portrayed the first example of the Spirit's power with his spine-tingling message, recorded in the second chapter of Acts. Upon hearing him, the people were profoundly moved: "When the people heard this, they were cut to the heart and said to Peter and the other apostles, 'Brethren, what shall we do?' " (Acts 2:37)

The Spirit's Sealing

As soon as a person puts his trust in Christ, he is *sealed* by the Holy Spirit (Eph. 1:13). The person is *secured* by the Spirit. A seal is a symbol of a finished transaction, of ownership, and of security.

We have *certainty and assurance of salvation* because we are sealed by the Spirit. We *know* we belong to the family of God: "The Spirit himself testifies with our spirit that we are God's children" (Rom. 8:16).

The Spirit indwells each individual Christian, each one's body is "the Spirit's temple." Jesus said, "Remain in me, and I will remain in you" (John 15:4). Our status is secure. Another time Jesus filled out the picture: "[The Spirit] lives *with* you and will be *in* you" (John 14:17, italics added).

We are sealed, indwelt, and baptized by the Holy Spirit *at the time we believe in Jesus Christ.* "For we were all baptized by one Spirit into one body—whether Jews or Greeks, slave or free—and we were all given the one Spirit" (1 Cor. 12:13). Baptism by the Spirit and not water is implicit. This baptism takes place at the time of conversion and only once. We are then sealed and indwelt by the Spirit. This is shared by every believer, despite varying degrees of maturity, strength, and devotion.

Filled with the Spirit

Speaking to the Ephesian Christians, Paul wrote, "Be filled with the Spirit" (Eph. 5:18). Being *filled* with the Spirit is not a once-for-all experience, but one He intends to be repeated. On the Day of Pentecost the disciples were filled with the Spirit (Acts 2:4). A few days later, in a dramatic prayer meeting, they had such an experience again (Acts 4:31).

The filling of the Spirit implies being given power and boldness for God's service, for strength to meet particular crises, or for everyday Spirit-led living. We experience renewal when we pray, "Lord, fill me today with your Spirit. Keep my eyes on you." The filling of the Spirit is an experience to be repeated as nec-

> **The Holy Spirit is a person, not a package on a string let down from heaven, nor is He a liquid and we a cup!**

essary in the life of each believer. The literal thought in Ephesians is "Keep on being filled."

The Holy Spirit is not a package on a string let down from heaven. He is not a liquid, nor are we a cup. He is a person. It follows then, that to "be filled" depends on our relationship to Him. It is not a matter of receiving more of Him but of *opening more of ourselves* to a certain and stronger relationship with Him. It is a matter of desiring Him to *more fully occupy, guide, and control every area of our lives.* Then, whatever life brings us, His power is more evident in us. His joy and peace control our emotions. Overall, He makes us effectively fruitful for Him.

Our inner thoughts and motives are guided when we are filled with the Spirit. All we are and have is subject to His control. The test as to whether or not you are filled with the Spirit is not "Have you received an external sign or been given a particular gift of the Spirit?" The test is rather "Have you given yourself wholly and without reservation to God?" (Rom. 12:1) Are you genuinely willing that He should control, absolutely and entirely, your life?

Many believers come to a point of utter frustration in their service for the Lord simply because they fail to realize the need to be filled with the Spirit if they are to act in God's power. Just as we cannot *save* ourselves apart from the work of the Holy Spirit, neither can we *live* the life of victory or serve the Lord effectively without the Spirit.

When we learn to trust Him fully and allow Him to work through us, He frees us from the frustration of trying to accomplish spiritual and eternal results solely through our human ability—or, more properly, inability.

It is the Holy Spirit who delivers us from the *power* of sin: "Through Christ Jesus the law of the Spirit of life set me free from the law of sin and death" (Rom. 8:2).

Through the Holy Spirit we *come* to know Christ, and by the Holy

Spirit's power we *live* and *grow* in Christ, in the service of the King and in the fellowship of His church. Paul gives an illuminating summary:

> *Be filled with the Spirit [keep on being filled],*
> *Speak to one another with psalms, hymns and spiritual*
> *songs,*
> *Sing and make music in your heart to the Lord,*
> *Always giving thanks to God the Father for everything,*
> *In the name of our Lord Jesus Christ. (Eph. 5:18-20)*

Salvation

From one point of view, salvation is very simple. It can be summed up in the Apostle Paul's straightforward words to the Philippian jailer: "Believe in the Lord Jesus, and you will be saved" (Acts 16:31).

At the same time, salvation is profound; it has the most pervasive and permanent impact possible on the one who experiences it. We do not, of course, have to understand all the aspects of salvation before we can receive it. We may understand very little when we first trust Jesus Christ. And there are some things we will not understand until we see God face-to-face. But studying God's Word and trying to understand more fully the truth of our salvation greatly enriches us spiritually.

Several theological, biblical terms are generally used in connection with salvation. Each contributes its own prism of truth and, taken together, they give a greater fullness of God's plan. None of these terms or truths can be isolated completely from the others. Each is best studied in the context of the entire message. There is no dogmatic *order or sequence* for them; they often overlap and may be different, yet corresponding views of the same truth.

Further, some truths are to be understood with the mind, and other truths are to be experienced personally in the heart. Both understanding and experience are involved.

Repentance

John the Baptist began his ministry with a call to *repentance:* "Repent, for the kingdom of heaven is near" (Matt. 3:2). Jesus began preaching with the identical words (Matt. 4:17). He commanded His disciples: "Repentance and forgiveness of sins will be preached in his name to all nations, beginning at Jerusalem" (Luke 24:47).

Peter also took up this message on the Day of Pentecost (Acts 2:38). Paul pointed out that now God "commands all people everywhere to repent." Acceptance of the Gospel means "both Jews and Greeks . . . must turn to God in repentance and have faith in our Lord Jesus" (Acts 20:21).

The word used in the Old Testament for *repentance* means "to turn or return." It implies a personal decision to turn away *from* sin and *to* God. In the New Testament, the terms *repent* and *repentance* apply to man's relationship to sin and God with the basic meaning of a "change of mind." The change of mind is about the reality of sin, and the decision to turn to God instead. In a sense, they are the negative and positive aspects of the same truth. The two together are inseparable and complementary. Paul, in his defense before Agrippa said: "I preached that they [Jews and Gentiles] should repent and turn to God and prove their repentance by their deeds" (Acts 26:20).

True repentance is not merely the feeling of remorse, such as Judas had after he betrayed the Lord. It involves the intellect, the emotions, and the will.

• *The intellect aids in repentance.* The intellect grasps the holiness of God and His law and our utter failure and inability to keep it. This is where repentance begins. Along with this, repentance may involve a "change of mind" as to *who Christ is.* This was true of the Jews on the Day of Pentecost (Acts 2:14-40). They had formerly viewed Jesus as an impostor, but Peter called on them to accept Him as Messiah and Savior.

• *The emotions are involved in repentance.* "Godly sorrow," in contrast to merely being superficially sorry for sin, frequently precedes the change of mind: "Godly sorrow brings repentance that leaves no regret." Eugene H. Peterson's *The Message* terms it "distress that drives us to God. . . . It turns us around" (2 Cor. 7:10). Repentance involves a feeling of the awfulness of sin in its destructive effect on the person and a breakup of his relationship to God. Repentance involves responding to the truth about ourselves: "A man doesn't call something crooked unless he has some idea of a straight line."

Emotion itself is no gauge of the genuineness of one's repentance. The presence or absence of tears does not necessarily indicate genuineness or lack of it. But when we truly repent, we are certain to experience some feeling about it even beginning with acknowledgment of our need for help.

• *The will plays a part in repentance.* The will makes the decision to repent. The Prodigal Son not only came to his senses intellectually and regretted what he had done, but he *acted:* "I will set out and go back to my father. . . . *So he got up and went to his father*" (Luke 15:18, 20, italics added). Repentance is a deliberate, willful turning away from sin and following after God. Genuine repentance always leads to a change in conduct and attitude.

Faith Is the Key

Repentance, if it is genuine, will lead to *faith.* In fact, some Christians understand faith to *include* repentance: "I've changed my mind." For a person to receive Christ as his or her Savior in faith is in itself evidence he or she has sinned and needs a Savior. The term *faith,* in its noun, verb, and adjective forms, is used dozens of times in the Old Testament, but it occurs several hundred times in the New Testament. Its most common meaning is "confident trust in or reliance on."

Faith is central to the whole Christian experience: "Without faith it is impossible to please God, because anyone who comes to him must believe that he exists and that he rewards those who earnestly seek him" (Heb. 11:6).

Faith, in the New Testament, always has as its background the person and work of Christ. He is the object of our faith, reliance, or trust: "Whoever believes in him shall not perish but have eternal life" (John 3:16). In and of itself, faith is meaningless. It always has an *object* to which it is directed and on which it rests. If the object of our faith is worthless, we are victims of superstition, no matter how sincerely we believe.

Ingredients of Saving Faith

• *The facts* about Christ—His deity, His death, and our need of Him—are the beginning of saving faith. We must accept these facts as *true*, however; mere mental assent to these truths does not save us. James makes this clear: "You believe that there is one God. Good! Even the demons believe that—and shudder" (James 2:19). One could not possibly be a Christian without believing the revealed facts about Jesus' identity.

• *Commitment and trust* in Christ, beyond a superficial belief *about* Christ to complete reliance on Him, are also key elements of saving faith. Such commitment and trust involve the *will* as well as the mind and the emotions. One does not believe simply because of one's feelings—one *decides* to believe. An example of this would be a person *deciding* to join another in marriage, forsaking all others and living with one particular person. Scripture uses this analogy also.

Faith is the instrument that links us to Christ. The New Testament emphasizes we are saved by *faith* and not by *works:* "However, to the man who does not work but trusts God who justifies the wicked, his faith is credited as righteousness" (Rom. 4:5).

At first sight, the Epistle of James appears to disagree: "What good is it, my brothers, if a man claims to have faith but has no deeds? Can such faith save him? . . . You see that a person is justified by what he does and not by faith alone" (James 2:14, 24).

The "faith" James criticizes is "head belief"—mere intellectual assent to facts. Such "faith" does not lead to holy living and hence is "dead" or "useless" (James 2:20). It has no saving value. When we read about "faith" in the other epistles, wholehearted trust in Christ is in view. On this kind of undivided faith God credits a believer with righteousness, leading its possessor to want a holy life.

• *Good works are the result of new life.* When we read that we are saved by faith rather than by "works," the works in view are the keeping of the Law in an effort to earn salvation. James (2:14, 18, 20) does not use the term *works* in this sense. His "works" are very much like "the fruit of the Spirit" of which Paul speaks (Gal. 5:22). This would be like a couple getting married but never seeing or contacting each other. There is no "fruit" to their marriage. Leon Morris points out, "Works are warm deeds of love springing from a right attitude to God. They are the fruits of faith. What James objects to is the claim that faith is there when there is no fruit to attest it."[1]

• *How does faith come about?* "Faith comes from hearing the message, and the message is heard through the word of Christ" (Rom. 10:17). In the days of the apostles, "many who heard the message believed" (Acts 4:4). God uses His Word, both spoken and written, to produce faith. At the same time, faith is a work of God. As we turn to Him, He is also drawing us.

In almost every phase of salvation, there is a mysterious interplay between the divine and human sides. It is not always possible, though, to draw neat lines of distinction. Two sides of the roof of a house may join together at the top, but the exact spot may be hidden in the clouds. Put simply, *repentance* and *faith* are man's response and then God acts.

Rebirth, a New Kind of Life

"Regeneration or the new birth is the divine side of that change of heart which, viewed from the human side, we call conversion."[2] Jesus' ungarnished statement to an intelligent inquirer put it simply, "No one can see the Kingdom of God unless he is born again." New life is essential.

This experience and reality is used to describe the act of God's Spirit to give us His kind of life inside, not making bad people good, but dead people alive. It is the renewal or rebirth of individuals: "He saved us, not because of righteous things we had done, but because of his mercy. He saved us through the washing of rebirth and renewal by the Holy Spirit" (Titus 3:5).

The seriousness and intransigence of sin is so deep, a person *cannot even see* the kingdom of God, let alone enter it, unless he is born from above, or born again (John 3:3).

> **New birth results not in a change of personality but in a whole new kind of life.**

These were Jesus' words in His conversation with the Jewish leader Nicodemus. God takes the initiative in renewal or rebirth, but man must actively respond in faith. "Yet to all who received him, to those who believed in his name, he gave the right to become children of God—children born not of natural descent, nor of human decision or a husband's will, but born of God" (John 1:12-13). "God, who is rich in mercy, made us alive with Christ even when we were dead in transgressions" (Eph. 2:4-5).

Before the new birth, self and sin are in control: "I'll do it my way." After renewal, the Holy Spirit is in control. A born-again person shares in the very life of God, participates in the "divine nature" (2 Peter 1:4), and is described as a "new creation" (2 Cor. 5:17). The person puts on "the new self, created to be like God in true righteousness and holiness" (Eph. 4:24; see also Col. 3:10). Rebirth is a decisive experience that happens once for all, then has continuing results in the life of a Christian. As C.S. Lewis puts it:

> What man, in his natural condition, has not got, is Spiritual life—the higher and different sort of life that exists in God. . . .

> And that is precisely what Christianity is about. This world is a great sculptor's shop. We are the statues and there is a rumor going round the shop that some of us are some day going to come to life . . . [alive to God].

> God became man to turn creatures into sons—not simply to produce better men of the old kind but to produce a new kind of man. Christ's work of making New Men [is like] . . . turning a horse into a winged creature. . . . It is not mere improvement but transformation.[3]

God "wants all men to be saved and to come to a knowledge of the truth" (1 Tim. 2:4). That some men are not reborn is not God's lapse. The responsibility rests with each of us. Jesus diagnosed this problem when speaking to a typical group, He said, "These are the scriptures that testify about me, yet you *refuse* to come to me to have life" (John 5:39-40, italics added). It wasn't that they *could* not have come, but that they *would* not. They deliberately refused to believe the message delivered to them.

How anyone actually comes to faith in Christ is a profound question. Some, by approaching the problem entirely from man's side, have tended to eclipse the sovereignty of God. Others, by approaching it only from God's side, have seemed to obliterate each individual's freedom.

We need to understand several theological terms to avoid confusion and popular misconceptions. These terms are *election*, *predestination*, and *foreknowledge*.

• *Election* implies God chooses only specific groups and people to receive His grace. This view is based on His sovereign pleasure and not on the value, goodness, or disposition of those chosen. In the Old Testament, God's election is illustrated in His choice of Abraham, with whom He made an everlasting covenant, and also in His choice to have a special relationship with Abraham's descendants, the nation of Israel (Gen. 11:31–12:7).

Election, as used in the New Testament, has to do with God's choice of particular individuals for salvation. Jesus said, "And he will send his angels and gather his elect from the four winds" (Mark 13:27). Christians are "chosen [elected] according to the foreknowledge of God the Father" (1 Peter 1:2). God "chose [elected] us in him before the creation of the world. . . . In love he predestined us to be adopted as his sons through Jesus Christ, in accordance with his pleasure and will" (Eph. 1:4-5). Jesus Himself explicitly said, "You did not choose me, but I chose you" (John 15:16).

• *Predestination* is a term used only of Christians. It indicates that God's purpose for a believer—that he become Christlike—is certain to be fulfilled. "For those God foreknew he also predestined to be conformed to the likeness of his Son. . . . And . . . those he called, he also justified; those he justified, he also glorified" (Rom. 8:29-30).

Foreknowledge, predestination, calling, justification, and glorification are all grouped together in one "package." A person who has *one* of them has them *all*. The sequence indicates that apart from the predetermination of God, we cannot trust in Christ. Jesus said, "No one can come to me unless the Father who

> # Election and predestination are always to salvation and its blessings— never to judgment.

sent me draws him" (John 6:44).

Like election, *predestination* is according to God's sovereign purpose and will. It is not based on any merits in those persons whom He has chosen.

It is important to realize that *all* men are sinners and are under the judgment of God:

> God in sovereign freedom treats some sinners as they deserve . . . but He selects others to be "objects of His mercy," receiving the "riches of His glory" (Rom. 9:23). This discrimination involves no injustice, for the All-Holy Creator owes mercy to none and has a right to do as He pleases with His rebellious creatures (Rom. 9:14-21). The wonder is not that He withholds mercy from some, but that He should be gracious to any.[4]

The purpose of the Bible's teaching on election and predestination is to lead pardoned sinners to worship God for the grace they have experienced. They come to see, in unmistakable terms, that salvation is *all* of God and not of themselves. They also come to see that since they were chosen in Christ before the foundation of the world, their election is eternal and therefore certain. This inspires devotion and love to Christ in gratitude for God's unfathomable love.

No one in hell will be able to tell God, "I wanted to be saved, but my name was on the wrong list." It is true that no one believes on the Savior unless God the Holy Spirit convicts him, but it is also true that those who do not trust Christ choose not to believe. *God never refuses to save anyone who wants salvation.*

• *Foreknowledge* of God means that God elects those to salvation whom He knows in advance will respond positively to the Gospel. Foreknowledge is not the same thing as foreordination or election. God's view is different than ours. He knows the end from the beginning. Dr. D.G. Barnhouse likened it to seeing a small piece of rug on the floor. We see the whole thing—all four edges of the piece of rug. We are above and outside the piece. God's view of our lives and time embraces the entire span since God is before and outside of all time.

Throughout church history, honest differences of opinion have arisen about these complex and not-fully-explainable doctrines. Believers should be persuaded in their own minds about them and should show a charitable spirit toward those who differ.

A Calvinist and an Arminian Dialogue

A conversation in 1784 between Charles Simeon, a follower of Arminius who disbelieved in predestination, and John Wesley, who did believe in predestination, can help us understand the mystery of coming to faith.

SIMEON: Sir, I understand that you are called an Arminian; and I have sometimes been called a Calvinist; and therefore I suppose we are to draw daggers. But before I consent to begin the combat, with your permission, I will ask you a few questions. . . . Pray, Sir, do you feel yourself a *depraved creature*, so depraved that you would never have thought of turning to God if God had not first put it in your heart?

WESLEY: Yes. I do indeed.

SIMEON: And do you utterly despair of recommending yourself to God by anything you can do, and look for salvation *solely through the blood and righteousness of Christ?*

WESLEY: Yes, solely through Christ.

SIMEON: But, Sir, supposing you were at first saved by Christ, are you not somehow or other to *save yourself* afterwards by your own works?

WESLEY: No, I must be saved by Christ from first to last.

SIMEON: Allowing, then, that you were first turned by the grace of God, are you not in some way or other to keep yourself by *your own power?*

WESLEY: No.

SIMEON: What then? Are you to *be upheld* every hour and every moment by God, as much as an infant in its mother's arms?

WESLEY: Yes, altogether.

SIMEON: And is *all your hope* in the grace and mercy of God to preserve you unto His heavenly kingdom?

WESLEY: Yes, I have no hope but in Him.

SIMEON: Then, Sir, with your leave I will put up my dagger again; for this is all my Calvinism; this is my election, my justification by faith, my final perseverance; it is in substance all that I hold, and as I hold it; and therefore, if you please, instead of searching out terms and phrases to be a ground of contention between us, we will *cordially unite* in those things wherein we agree.[5]

Justification: Declared Righteous

The experience of salvation, in relation to the divine and human factors, does contain ambiguities to our finite understanding. The *results* of salvation, however, are very clear. There are three extraordinary benefits referring to the aspects of salvation: past, present, and future.

> We have *been* saved (justification).
> We are *being* saved (sanctification).
> We *shall be* saved (glorification).

Justification has often been defined as meaning "Just as if I'd never sinned." This thought conveys forgiveness, acquittal of the past sin at the time of new birth. But justification goes even further by positively declaring a person to be *righteous*. When God justifies us, His forgiveness does not merely make us neutral—moral and spiritual zeroes. His forgiveness brings Him to look on us "in Christ," as *having His perfect righteousness*. He credits or assigns Christ's righteousness to the trusting person. This does not make one *personally* righteous, but it *declares* that person righteous in a *legal sense*, his debt has been paid, his sins have been forgiven, and he is brought into right relationship with God.

Paul stresses that we cannot be justified by the works of the law, for "no one will be declared righteous in [God's] sight by observing the Law; rather, through the law we become conscious of sin" (Rom. 3:20). He goes on to explain: "[We] are justified freely by [God's] grace through the redemption that came by Christ Jesus" (Rom. 3:24).

The *basis*, or ground, of our justification, or being declared righteous, is twofold.

• *Christ's death* as our substitute satisfied the claims of God's holy Law against our sin: "While we were still sinners, Christ died for us. Since we have now been justified by his blood, how much more shall we be saved from God's wrath through him!" (Rom. 5:8-9)

• *God assigns us Christ's righteousness*, based on His perfect obedience: "Just as through the disobedience of the one man [Adam] the many [all people] were made sinners, so also through the obedience of the one man [Christ] the many [all who believe] will be made righteous" (Rom. 5:19).

Christ became identified with us when He was made sin for us on the cross. When we believe, we are given His newness of resurrection life, and we share His righteousness.

Justification comes by faith. This truth burst upon the heart and mind of Martin Luther like a bombshell after a lengthy, unsuccessful struggle with self-flagellation to win God's favor. He saw the magnitude of the one truth: "The righteous will live by faith" (Rom. 1:17). He saw it was not what *he* could do to merit God's favor, but what *God* had already done for him at the cross. There Christ made justification and peace possible. The Protestant Reformation grew out of this discovery.

Evidence that we have been justified is seen in God *changing our lives, obeying Him,* and *desiring to do His will.* When we say we have been "saved," we are referring to our justification. Paul wrote to the Ephesians: "For it is by grace you have been saved, through faith" (Eph. 2:8). Paul's certainty of a past event, based on what God had done, led him to overflow with assurance. He wrote: "For I am convinced that neither death nor life, neither angels nor demons, neither the present nor the future, nor any powers, neither height nor depth, nor anything else in all creation, *will be able to separate us from the love of God that is in Christ Jesus our Lord*" (Rom. 8:38-39, italics added).

We too may enjoy such assurance, for our salvation is an accomplished fact if we are in Christ.

Sanctification: Ongoing Growth

In addition to being justified, we are also being saved, a process of becoming more like Jesus Christ, more holy. This is called *sanctification.*

Justification has to do with our standing before God and is instantaneous. Sanctification has to do with our ongoing growth in Christian character and conduct and is progressive. It continues as long as we live.

Sanctification is a process. Basically, the word *sanctified* means "set apart." The term *saint* comes from the same root and means "a set-apart one" to the Lord. Another word with the same meaning is *holy*. *Sanctify* is used in two ways.

• *Sanctify* means to be set apart, or declared holy, for God's use or service. Christians are called "saints" in this sense—God has set them apart for His service. Such "sanctification" is usually regarded as being instantaneous and as taking place at the time of one's conversion: "You were washed, you were sanctified, you were justified in the name of the Lord Jesus Christ and by the Spirit of our God" (1 Cor. 6:11).

• *Sanctify* means to make the personal life of an individual Christian holy, in the sense of moral and spiritual improvement. This is a lifelong process. We are to "grow in the grace and knowledge of our Lord and Savior Jesus Christ" (2 Peter 3:18), and as we mature spiritually we are "transformed into [Christ's] likeness with ever-increasing glory, which comes from the Lord, who is the Spirit" (2 Cor. 3:18).

Some feel that sanctification is a crisis experience, as is justification, and that one can experience "entire sanctification" in a moment of time. Differences of opinion on this question hinge almost completely on the definition of sin versus holy living. *Sin* is often defined as "any voluntary transgression of a known law," as Wesley put it. The Westminster Shorter Catechism, on the other hand, defines *sin* as "any want of conformity unto or transgression of the Law of God." This definition includes sins of omission as well as overt sins committed deliberately.

How does God sanctify? Those who say the process of sanctification is all of God tend to minimize human responsibility. On the other hand, those who tend to minimize sin exaggerate human responsibility in sanctification.

Both *God's initiative and man's responsibility* are expressed in the scriptural command: "Continue to work out your salvation with fear and trembling, for it is God who works in you to will and to act according to his good purpose" (Phil. 2:12-13). Because God works in a people, they are able to do any good work. On the other hand, although God enables, people must respond. They are to show neither supine passivity nor naive confidence in their own efforts. God is the apex of a Christian's sanctification.

God's command is: "Live by the Spirit, and you will not gratify the desires of the sinful nature" (Gal. 5:16). The Holy Spirit gives us power to overcome sin and produces in us the fruit of the Spirit (Gal. 5:22-23). This "walk" is a life of daily faith in which we claim what has already been given us by God, and then we live by it. Christ has been made to us "wisdom, [and] righteousness, holiness and redemption" (1 Cor. 1:30).

Justification: God declares us righteous.

Sanctification: God delivers us daily from the power of sin.

Glorification: God delivers us from the presence of sin in heaven.

As we depend on Christ, then, His patience, love, power, purity, etc. will begin to show in our attitudes and conduct. He does not dole out these qualities to us in "little packages"—we have all of them we need in Christ, who indwells us. "His divine power has given us everything we need for life and godliness through our knowledge of him who called us by his own glory and goodness" (2 Peter 1:3).

The key principle in sanctification, as in justification, is faith, i.e., confident trust and reliance on Jesus Christ. We can be *saved* only by faith, and we can *live effectively* as Christians only by faith: "Just as you received Christ Jesus as Lord [by faith], continue to live in him" (Col. 2:6). God, in both instances, does what we cannot do. Our part is to respond in faith.

Glorification: Future Sinlessness

Salvation, in one sense, is also future: we *shall* be saved. We have been saved from the *power* of sin; and we shall be saved from the very *presence* of sin when we see Him face-to-face. We shall personally be perfect and free from all sin. It is in this sense that we are appointed "to *receive* salvation" (1 Thess. 5:9), and it is this salvation that is ready to be revealed in the last days and about which Paul refers when he writes that "our salvation is nearer now than when we first believed" (Rom. 13:11). This complete and final sanctification, this deliverance from the very presence of sin, is called *glorification*.

"Dear friends, now we are children of God, and what we will be has not yet been made known. But we know that when he appears, we shall be like him, for we shall see him as he is" (1 John 3:2).

Salvation is God's great gift to man. In experience, its many aspects may not be separated, but an understanding of these details gives Christians deeper appreciation, greater love, and happier praise for the God who has saved them.

Angels, Satan, and Demons

A ngels are getting an overflow of attention today from every quarter. Cards, gifts, jewelry, art, and knickknacks of every kind tout winged creatures. People use the term "guardian angel," amplified as "my own personal guardian angel," sincerely and seriously.

We also know that some tribal peoples worship, pray to, and fear demons and evil spirits. Are angels, the Devil, and demons the result of ignorant superstition, or are they objective realities? Current popular views can affect Christians and non-Christians alike and entice us all, victimizing us with erroneous, even harmful ideas. Again, the Bible is our avenue for trustworthy answers about spiritual beings of any kind.

Angels Are Messengers

Angels are mentioned more than 250 times in both the Old and the New Testaments. Jesus Himself referred to them many times. The Greek term translated *angel* literally means "messenger." Angels are basically *messengers or servants* of God. Their message is God's might, power, and care

(2 Thess. 1:7).

In some Old Testament passages the title "the angel of the Lord" appears to be identified with God but is *never confused with God*. There is an obvious distinction.

It is quite easy to see how angels can become a focus of praise. There is a kind of benign, loving feeling about their profile. Yet the true characteristics of God's compassion and grace are far greater than an army of angels.

Suppose, for instance, you received a gift someone sent you by express mail. The driver rang the doorbell, handed you the package, and started to turn away. But you reached out and began to embrace him, thank him, and invite him in for coffee. He, the messenger, was so generous, you thought. Obviously, you would not do this. The *sender* is the one you would thank, not the delivery man. The same is true with angels. The Father in heaven is the Giver of all good gifts, the source of mercy and blessing. Wonderful verses tell us of angels as messengers of His compassion: "Every good and perfect gift is from above, coming down from the Father of the heavenly lights, who does not change like shifting shadows" (James 1:17). "For he will command his angels concerning you to guard you in all your ways" (Ps. 91:11).

The Bible describes angels as seeing the face of God and as regularly in His presence (Matt. 18:10), but the word *guardian* is not used in Scripture—there is no mention of "our own personal guardian angel." Most poignant are the words of Jesus speaking about "little ones." He said, "Their angels in heaven always see the face of my Father" (Matt. 18:10).

Concerning Jesus' return to earth in the last days, He said, "No one knows about that day or hour, not even the angels in heaven" (Mark 13:32). Other references Jesus made to angels are recorded in Mark 8:38 and Matthew 13:41; 26:53.

Attributes of Angels

• *Angels are created beings* as we know from these words describing Jesus: "For by him [Jesus] all things were created: things in heaven and on earth, visible and invisible, whether thrones or powers or rulers or authorities; all things were created by him and for him" (Col. 1:16).

Angels preceded man in creation. The words "In the beginning God created the heavens and the earth" would undoubtedly include the creation of angels, though they are not specifically mentioned.

• *Angels are spirit beings*, not like human beings, who have both body and spirit. Nowhere does the Bible ever mention, as it does about us, that angels have the "image of God." Angels are different than the human race and do not "inherit salvation." Angels are incorporeal spirit beings, and have no bodies as we do: "Are not all angels ministering spirits sent to serve those who will inherit salvation?" (Heb. 1:14) They at times *take bodily form*, as when two angels came to Lot in Sodom (Gen. 19:1), and sometimes they become visible, as at the Resurrection (John 20:12). Such appearances, however, are exceptions rather than the rule.

• *The masculine gender* is always used with the word *angel*, however, there is no mention of sexual orientation with these beings. Jesus implied this when He said of resurrected believers, "At the resurrection people will neither marry nor be given in marriage; they will be like the angels in heaven" (Matt. 22:30).

• *Eternal beings*, angels never die. They are not subject to aging, and in heaven we shall be like them in this respect: "[the saved in heaven] can no longer die; for they are like the angels" (Luke 20:35).

• *Higher than men* in God's order of creation, angels are not gods. God made man a little *lower* than the angels (Ps. 8:5). Redeemed man, however, as part of the new creation God has promised, will be higher than the angels and at that time man will have authority over them: "Do you not know that we will judge angels?" (1 Cor. 6:3)

• *The intelligence of angels* is greater than man's, though they are limited spirits, not God. This truth is implied in our Lord's statement that the angels, though they are in heaven, do not know the day or the hour of the end time (Mark 13:32). The Gospel and salvation are things the angels "long to look into" (1 Peter 1:12).

• *Angels excel in strength physically* (Ps. 103:20). One angel was able to kill 185,000 Assyrians in one night (Isa. 37:36). Again, angels' power is not theirs inherently, but comes completely by delegation from God.

• *Angels stand in the very presence of God*. As mentioned, Jesus said they "always see the face of my Father" (Matt. 18:10). In this respect, they are higher than men and continually *worship God* (Rev. 5:11-12; Isa. 6:3). They also *take pleasure in His works and grace,* and *show awareness of human beings* and interest in our individual well-being: "There is rejoicing in the presence of the angels of God over one sinner who repents" (Luke 15:10).

Angelic Activity

The activity of angels on earth has a number of facets, though essentially it is concerned with doing God's will: "You his angels . . . who obey his word. . . . You his servants who do his will" (Ps. 103:20-21).

1. *Angel's relate to individual believers.*

• They protected Daniel because of his faithfulness to God. To the amazed Darius, who appeared at the lion pit expecting to find him dead, Daniel said, "My God sent his angel, and he shut the mouths of the lions. They have not hurt me" (Dan. 6:22).

• Elijah was distraught and hungry and an angel provided for his physical need for food and encouraged His spirit: "[An] angel . . . touched him and said, 'Get up and eat' " (1 Kings 19:5).

• Peter was twice released from prison by an angel (Acts 5:19; 12:8-11). From these instances and others, we see how angels defend, protect, and deliver God's servants when it is in His providence to do so.

• Philip was guided to witness to an unbeliever as the angel directed him co approach the Ethiopian (Acts 8:26). Angels may likewise direct a Christian to a specific unbeliever today. Angels may also guide the unbeliever to approach a Christian, as when the angel instructed Cornelius to "bring back a man called Peter."

• In the midst of a shipboard crisis, Paul was cheered by an angel in the night (Acts 27:23). During His agony in the garden, our Lord Himself was strengthened by an angel (Luke 22:43).

• Luke 16 relates the story of a beggar who died and "the angels carried him" to heaven to be with God. This activity can be comforting for us at the death of a loved one.

2. *Angels are concerned with the church and its activity.* Paul charged Timothy, concerning his ministry: "I charge you, in the sight of God and Christ Jesus and the elect angels, to keep these instructions" (1 Tim. 5:21).

3. *Angels will accompany Christ when He comes in clouds of glory.* "When the Son of man comes . . . and all the angels with him, he will sit on his throne in heavenly glory" (Matt. 25:31).

How Many Angels?

Scripture does not list the number of the angels, but it is clear that they are many. Daniel, of his vision of God, said, *"Thousands upon thousands* attended him; ten thousand times ten thousand stood before him" (Dan. 7:10, italics added). John reported of *his* vision: "I looked and heard the voice of many angels, numbering thousands upon thousands, and ten thousand times ten thousand" (Rev. 5:11).

> **Christians should never fail to sense the operation of an angelic glory. It forever eclipses the world of demonic powers, as the sun does a candle's light.**

Among this vast number of angels there is organization and rank. Jesus said that had He so desired, He could have summoned more than twelve legions of angels (Matt. 26:53). References to the hosts of heaven in the Old Testament imply organization. Micaiah, a prophet, said, "I saw the Lord sitting on his throne with all the host of heaven standing around him on his right and on his left" (1 Kings 22:19).

The statement about "thrones or powers or rulers or authorities" in Colossians 1:16 seems to indicate ranking. These orders of heavenly beings are viewed as good, being God-ordained.

Evil beings seem to have similar organization and ranking: "Our struggle is not against flesh and blood, but against the rulers, against the authorities, against the powers of this dark world and against *the spiritual forces of evil in the heavenly realms*" (Eph. 6:12, italics added).

Other Angelic Beings

Michael is one of two angels whose name we know. He is an archangel, considered a special guardian of Israel and as "one of the chief princes" (Dan. 10:13, 21). He contended with the Devil for the body of Moses (Jude 9). It may have been Michael who spoke to Moses on Mount Sinai, or Horeb (Ex. 3:2). He led the battle in heaven against Satan (Rev. 12:7).

Gabriel is the only other angel named in the Bible. He is renowned for blowing his horn. Presumably this association comes from 1 Thessalonians 4:16, where Christ's return is said to be accompanied by "the voice of the archangel and with the trumpet call of God." Gabriel appears in the Old Testament as the one commissioned to explain the meaning of Daniel's vision of a ram and a he-goat (Dan. 8:16) and to declare to him the prophecy of the seventy weeks (9:21-27).

In the New Testament he announced two great births—of John to Zechariah and Elizabeth and of Jesus to Mary (Luke 1:19, 26-33). Gabriel evidently has high rank as one who continually stands in the very presence of the Lord (Luke 1:19). His function seems to be that of a *messenger*, while Michael appears to be that of a *warrior*.

Over the centuries many misconceptions about angels have developed. We have strayed far from the biblical concept of angels.

Never Mediators

Angels are never mediators between people and God, and we are not to worship them. Certain ancient Greek philosophers developed a whole series of graded emanations or spirits through which men could make contact with God. These philosophers maintained that God is much too holy to have anything to do with material things in general, and with earth and man in particular. Ancient Zoroastrianism taught a similar belief.

This sort of doctrine is totally foreign to the Bible's teaching, however. Angels are God's messengers, but this in no way implies that He has no direct contact with men when He so chooses. We approach God through no other way but Jesus Christ. No celestial being or person could be more compassionate and approachable than our God: "There is one God and one mediator between God and men, the man Christ Jesus, who gave himself as a ransom" (1 Tim. 2:5-6).

What, No Wings?

In most popular thinking and art, angels are winged creatures. There is little biblical warrant for this notion. In Scripture, angels are always described as appearing in masculine form.

Cherubim and seraphim (the plural form of cherub and seraph) are the only winged beings mentioned in Scripture. We do not have a great deal of information about either. God stationed *cherubim* at the east entrance of the Garden of Eden with a flaming sword to guard the tree of life (Gen. 3:24). In Ezekiel's vision (1:5; 10:1ff), cherubim are called "living creatures." Each cherub is described as having four faces—of man, lion, ox, and eagle. Each has four wings: two are stretched upward and two downward to cover his body.

Seraphim are mentioned only in Isaiah's vision of the heavenly temple. They have six wings and can fly (Isa. 6:2, 6). These beings apparently were human in form, apart from their wings, and were associated with the cherubim in guarding the divine throne. It is possible that the cherubim and seraphim are in some way related to the living creatures, angels, in heaven (Rev. 4–5).

People do not become angels after they die. Contrary to a popular mythology, there is absolutely no scriptural warrant for this idea.

Do Angels Appear Today?

The question often arises as to whether angels appear today as they did in biblical times. Experience does not indicate that such appearances are usual. There is, however, no biblical teaching that *rules out* this possibility. It would be wise, however, to maintain an attitude of healthy skepticism toward any story of an angelic appearance, unless the report was independently verified. Sometimes people embellish their stories unwittingly in retelling them.

One story about angels which seems to be authentic has to do with the well-known missionary to the New Hebrides, John G. Paton.

Since he had aroused the enmity of the local native chief by his successes in the Gospel, the chief

> **People do not become angels when they die.**

hired a man to kill the missionary. The man went to the missionary's house, but instead of murdering Paton he returned in terror,
saying he had seen a row of men, dressed in white, surrounding the
missionary's home. The chief thought the man had drunk too much
whiskey and encouraged him to try again. The next time others of
the tribe accompanied him. That night they all saw three rows of
men surrounding Paton's home.

When the chief asked the missionary where he kept the men in
the daytime who surrounded his house at night, Paton, knowing
nothing of what had happened, disclaimed the whole idea. When
the chief, in amazement, told his story, the missionary realized the
natives had seen an angelic company which God had sent to protect him, and he related it to Psalm 34:7: "The angel of the Lord
encamps around those who fear him [God], and he delivers them."
The savages were powerfully impressed with the missionary's explanation, as well they might be.[1]

Evil Spiritual Beings

God created angels perfect, and they were originally uncorrupted in spirit. At the same time, they had *free will* and were susceptible to *temptation
and sin.* How sin could have come into the experience of a perfect creature is a mystery, but that it actually happened is clear. The serpent,
called "crafty," who visited the Garden of Eden to tempt man was used
by the Devil or Satan to incite God's creatures against Him.

Peter supports his warnings against false prophecy and apostasy by
recalling God's judgment on angels (2 Peter 2:4), and Jude writes of
angels who "did not keep their positions of authority" (Jude 6). The
cause and time of the angels' fall is not specified, but it obviously included the fall of Satan plus other angels.

Satan Does Exist

The name *Satan* means "adversary" or "opponent." Peter calls him "your
enemy the devil" (1 Peter 5:8). Joshua stood before the angel of the Lord,
with "Satan standing at his right side to accuse him" (Zech. 3:1). Satan
is the opposer and enemy of both God and His people.

Some consider belief in the existence and personality of Satan as primitive, naive, even superstitious. Some consider Satan only a personification of the evil in the world. This notion has resulted partly from reaction to extravagant ideas and poetic expressions about Satan that were prominent during the Middle Ages. But these distorted ideas have no basis in Scripture, our only source of authoritative information.

> **Satan is the opposer and adversary of God and His people. He does not have a red suit, tail, and pitchfork.**

Nowhere does the Bible depict Satan as wearing a red suit with horns, a tail, and a pitchfork. It could be that caricatures are part of Satan's wiles to persuade sophisticated people that he doesn't exist.

Biblically, there can be no doubt as to the Devil's existence and personality. He is presented as appearing before the Lord, challenging him about Job (Job 1:6-12; 2:1-7). There is no mistaking Satan's reality in his temptation of our Lord in the wilderness. He spoke to Jesus and Jesus spoke to him (Matt. 4:1-11).

Satan has many other names. His other scriptural names confirm his reality and personality. The only other proper name given him is *Devil*. Other terms applied to him describe him and his work. He is *the tempter* (1 Thess. 3:5). He is the *evil one* who snatches the good seed of the Word of God from people's hearts (Matt. 13:19). He is our *enemy* (1 Peter 5:8). Jesus calls him the *father of lies* and a *murderer* (John 8:44). He is the supreme *deceiver* (Rev. 12:9).

Belial (2 Cor. 6:15) and *Beelzebub* (Matt. 12:24) have obscure derivations, but are used as synonyms for Satan. They denote a wicked person.

Demon Possession

There are some theologians who regard demon possession as only a primitive, prescientific description of what we now call mental illness. Doubtless, in the past, some victims of mental illness have been wrongly accused of demon possession and treated harshly. Wisdom should cause us to guard against confusion of the two conditions.

One view regards all sickness as initiated and caused by demons, but the New Testament draws definite distinctions between sickness and demon possession: "People brought to him all who were ill with various diseases, those suffering severe pain, the demon-possessed, those having seizures, and the paralyzed, and he healed them" (Matt. 4:24). Here differentiation is made between ordinary diseases and demon possession, and between demon possession and dementia.

On another occasion, Jesus cast out a demon who had caused dumbness (Matt. 9:32-33). From this account it is clear that the results of demon possession are not exclusively mental or nervous. Nor does the Bible connect epilepsy with demon possession. The boy Jesus healed of fits (Matt. 17:15-18) seems to have been afflicted with more than epilepsy. The Gerasene maniac (Mark 5:1-20), in addition to being demon-possessed, may also have been mentally ill.

Demon possession is seldom mentioned in the Old Testament, the Book of Acts, or the Epistles. The incidents of it centered around our Lord's ministry and may indicate a special attack on mankind by Satan during that period.

Demon possession is a worldwide phenomenon, however, with authenticated contemporary cases being reported in the United States as well as in other parts of the world. It is indeed possible to open oneself deliberately to demons. Trifling with the occult or playing around the edges of the spirit world are dangerous practices, and Christians should carefully avoid them.

The Christian's Perspective on Satan

We cannot conquer demons by our own power. Even the disciples had some frustrating encounters with such spirits. Jesus said, "This kind can come out only by prayer" (Mark 9:29). Generally, evil spirits were exorcised by being commanded to come out in the name of Christ (Acts 16:18). It has been suggested that rather than attempt to exorcise a satanic spirit ourselves, even in the name of Christ, we should ask God to do it for us as Michael, the archangel, did in a dispute with the Devil. He simply said, "The Lord rebuke you" (Jude 9).

Despite the great power of Satan and his demons, however, Christians need not fear them if they are in close fellowship with the Lord. The reality of the Holy Spirit's presence in us ensures our safety (1 John 4:4).

Several truths are clear from scriptural teachings and their implications about Satan and demons.

1. Satan's power over a believer is limited. The Devil could not touch Job without God's permission (Job 1:9-12; 2:4-6). Demons had to ask permission of Christ to enter swine (Mark 5:12). Satan is *not* all-powerful.

2. Neither is the Devil all-knowing. If he were, he would have known in advance the futility of his scheme to subvert Job, and he would surely have realized that it was useless for him to tempt the Lord in the wilderness.

3. Satan was conquered by Christ. John wrote, "The reason the Son of God appeared was to destroy the devil's work" (1 John 3:8).

4. Satan is slated for final judgment: "And the devil, who deceived them, was thrown into the lake of burning sulfur, where the beast and the false prophet had been thrown. They will be tormented day and night for ever and ever" (Rev. 20:10).

A Christian's Defense Against Satan

The Lord Jesus Christ has overcome Satan at the cross; therefore, Christians can claim God's promise of help when they resist the Devil, causing him to flee (James 4:7). But our resistance must be "standing firm in the faith" (1 Peter 5:9). We can best thwart Satan's designs on us by daily yielding ourselves to the Lord in prayer and by putting on the whole armor of God (Eph. 6:10-17).

We can also defend ourselves against Satan in other ways.

• We can avoid the extreme of trying to see Satan behind every misfortune without recognizing our personal responsibility and choice for our actions.

• Equally dangerous, however, is being so lulled by the sophistication of our age that we are unaware of Satan and his wiles against us in the spiritual battle in which every true believer is engaged.

• We can develop a "renewed mind" by knowing biblical principles (Rom. 12:2).

• We can avoid tempting circumstances or dabbling around the edges of things that seem harmless: "Let no one be found among you . . . who practices divination or sorcery, interprets omens, engages in witchcraft, or casts spells, or who is a medium or spiritist or who consults the dead" (Deut. 18:10-11).

• We should test Ouija boards, tarot cards, computer games, TV shows, and movies, to see if they be of God: "Test the spirits to see whether they are from God" (1 John 4:1).

• We can use Michael's phrase: "The Lord rebuke you" when temptation comes.

• When we run the Christian race for all we're worth, we won't have time for Satan and his world. The writer of Hebrews tells us, "Let us run with perseverance the race marked out for us. Let us fix our eyes on Jesus, the author and perfecter of our faith, who for the joy set before him endured the cross, scorning its shame, and sat down at the right hand of the throne of God" (Heb. 12:1-2). Then we can see angels and other spirit beings in their right perspective.

Billy Graham aptly summarizes, "Angels spell out the tenderness of God's love, meet a desperate need; then they are gone. Angels never draw attention to themselves but ascribe glory to God and press His message upon the hearers as a delivering and sustaining word of the highest order. They are vigorous in delivering the heirs of salvation from the stratagems of evil."[2]

The Church

I n only three decades following the death, resurrection, and ascension of Jesus Christ into heaven, His disciples had fanned out to Greece, Rome, and beyond. By A.D. 60 there were small congregations meeting together regularly from Jerusalem to Rome. Their message was impacting both Jews and Gentiles.

The dominant religion outside the Hebrew world embraced a vast array of gods and goddesses, largely remote and uninvolved in human affairs. The story of the Man from Galilee began to grow, sometimes through one-on-one witnessing (Paul was guarded by a Roman soldier for two years) and sometimes through dynamic public messages in public forums. By the turn of the century, A.D. 100, some scholars tell us the followers of this new "church" had grown to 10 percent of the Roman population.

The Christian believers met regularly and "joined together constantly in prayer" from the beginning. Acts chapter 1 records *120* of them meeting together. Chapter 2 mentions that *3,000* were added to the group, and chapter 4 puts the number of believers at *5,000* (Acts 1:14-15; 2:41;

4:4). This practice of joining together was what Jesus had called "the church."

In the New Testament, the Greek word *ekklesia,* translated "church," refers to a "called out" group, or "assembly," a word used regularly for secular gatherings of any kind. The Ephesus town clerk, trying to quell a near-riot, said, "If there is anything further you want to bring up, it must be settled in a legal assembly *[ekklesia]*" (Acts 19:39).

People—Not Buildings

Applied to Christians, *ekklesia* meant the church—"those who have been called out to Jesus Christ." According to D.W.B. Robinson, it "mostly means *a local congregation of Christians and never a building.*"[1]

God has always had His people. From the time of the Fall, when God gave Adam and Eve His promise of the Redeemer (Gen. 3:15), all who have believed His promises have been His people. *"His people" is an excellent definition of church.*

God called Abraham and promised him, "all peoples on earth will be blessed through you" (Gen. 12:3). God established an eternal covenant with the nation of Israel as His "chosen people." They were not chosen because of inherent superiority over other racial or ethnic groups, as poignantly described in Deuteronomy 7:7-8: "The Lord did not set his affection on you and choose you because you were more numerous than other peoples, for you were the fewest of all peoples. But it was because the Lord loved you and kept the oath he swore to your forefathers."

Merely being born into the nation of Israel did not make a person one of God's people spiritually: "A man is not a Jew if he is only one *outwardly,* nor is circumcision merely outward and physical. No, a man is a Jew if he is one *inwardly*; and circumcision is circumcision of the heart, by the Spirit, not by the written code" (Rom. 2:28-29, italics added). Many who were not Jews physically became *Jews spiritually* by recognizing Jehovah as the true and living God and turning from idols to Him.

Perhaps the most dramatic example of conversion to Judaism was in the days of Esther, after God's deliverance of the Jews from Haman, the Persian villain bent on massacring them: "In every province and in every city, wherever the edict of the king went, there was joy and gladness among the Jews, with feasting and celebrating. And many people of other nationalities became Jews" (Es. 8:17). The occasion is still celebrated today at the Feast of Purim.

God's People Described

The church was first mentioned by Jesus: "On this rock I will build my church, and the gates of Hades will not overcome it" (Matt. 16:18). He used the word a second time in Matthew 18:17, instructing His fol-

> **The church was Jesus' idea, not man's.**

lowers to take disputes to the "church" as the place to arbitrate disagreements between Christians or others. The plan originated in His mind, and He described the simplest form of a church: "For where two or three come together in my name, there am I with them" (Matt. 18:20).

Then, beginning with Acts 2:47, the rest of the New Testament uses "church" constantly when referring to the collective gathering of the Christians.

The New Testament church, then, is defined in two ways.

• It is *worldwide*, "the whole company of regenerate persons . . . in heaven and on earth" (Matt. 16:18; Eph. 5:24-25; Heb. 12:23).[2] This is the universal, invisible church. It is universal, including all true believers in every place, those who have gone on as well as those still alive. It is invisible, in that it includes all believers in Jesus Christ apart from a visible gathering: "God placed all things under his [Christ's] feet and appointed him to be head over everything for the church, which is his body" (Eph. 1:22-23).

• It is also the *individual local group, or church*—the group you belong to and the group I belong to. Strong writes, "The individual church may be defined as that smaller company of regenerate persons who, in any given community, unite themselves voluntarily together in accordance with Christ's laws, for the purpose of securing the complete establishment of His kingdom in themselves and in the world."[3]

Again, the church is *people—not buildings*. Today we use the word *church* in several additional ways. In answer to the question, "Where is your church?" we are more likely to answer, "At 18th and Green Streets" than "At County Hospital," "Joe's Texaco Station," "Motorola," or "Circle Campus."

Really a church is where its members are at any given time. Part of our problem, in reaching the world today, results from our "building" mentality. When we think of the activities of the church, we tend to think only of what goes on within the four walls of the church building, rather than what takes place *in the world* through what believers *say, do,* and *are.*

The Church Born in Jerusalem

The Christian *ekklesia* was born in Jerusalem with the coming of the Holy Spirit on the Day of Pentecost; that day could be called its birthday. After Peter's sermon on that occasion, "Those who accepted his message were baptized, and about three thousand were added to their number that day" (Acts 2:41). At first it consisted mainly of Jews who recognized Jesus as the Messiah. Many of

> The church has a double purpose: gathering Christians in and sending them out to spread Jesus Christ's message.

them were Hellenists—that is, Greek-speaking Jews—who had been scattered all over the empire, yet many Jews regularly came to Jerusalem as pilgrims.

The church was then considered a sect within Judaism. One of Paul's accusers referred to him as "a troublemaker, stirring up riots among the Jews all over the world. He is a ringleader of the Nazarene sect" (Acts 24:5). The Roman government gave Christians the same exemption from military service it gave the Jews. The first Jewish Christians in Jerusalem continued to recognize their obligations to the Mosaic Law and still participated in the worship services of the temple or synagogue.

Not Built on Favoritism

Increasingly, however, *Jewish proselytes* (Gentiles who had embraced Judaism) believed the Gospel and came into the church. After all, Jesus' message began with "God so loved the *world.*" Philip preached the Good News in Samaria and later baptized an Ethiopian to whom he had witnessed (Acts 8). Only after a vision from the Lord did the universal scope of the Gospel finally get through to reluctant Peter (Acts 10:9-16). He later explained to Cornelius, a Gentile, that it had been "against our law for a Jew to associate with a Gentile or visit him. But God has shown me that I should not call any man impure or unclean" (v. 28).

On hearing Cornelius' declaration of faith, Peter uttered this historic words: "I now realize how true it is that God does not show favoritism but accepts men from every nation who fear him and do what is right" (vv. 34-35).

As if to vouch for the truth of what Peter was saying, the Holy Spirit came on his listeners, most of whom were Gentiles, as he spoke. The Jews with Peter were amazed that Gentiles also received the Holy Spirit. Then Peter baptized the new Gentile believers.

Other Christian Jews preached the Gospel in Antioch, where a mixed church of Jews and Gentiles came into existence (Acts 13:1). It was here in Antioch that believers were *first called Christians or "Christ's men"* (Acts 11:26). Should the Gentile converts have to keep the Jewish laws, circumcision, and food requirements? The church held a council in Jerusalem and then made the momentous declaration: "It seemed good to the Holy Spirit and to us not to burden you with anything beyond the following requirements: You are to abstain from food sacrificed to idols, from blood, from the meat of strangled animals and from sexual immorality. You will do well to avoid these things" (Acts 15:28-29).

Three New Testament Pictures

The metaphors used for the church in the New Testament teach its multifunctions for believers.

1. The church is the *"body of Christ."* Jesus Christ Himself is the *Head* of the body. Every member functions under the leadership of the Head and with interdependence upon other members: "The body is a unit, though it is made up of many parts; and though all its parts are many, they form one body. So it is with Christ" (1 Cor. 12:12; see also Eph. 4:4; Col. 3:15).

Christ leads the church, and it is to be subject to Him (Eph. 5:23-24). He is the source of its unity: "for you are all one in Christ Jesus" (Gal. 3:28).

Every part of the body is important. As in the physical body, even the smallest part is as significant as the largest. The unknown woman and man who pray are as important as the more visible teacher. When one suffers the whole body suffers. "There should be no division in the body" for each part is needed (1 Cor. 12:25).

Members of the church are to have an intimate relationship with each other as well as with Christ; therefore, what hurts one member will hurt all, and when one member is honored, all the others will rejoice with him (1 Cor. 12:26).

2. The church is *the building of God:* "You also, like living stones, are being built into a spiritual house to be a holy priesthood" (1 Peter 2:5). This household of God is "built on the foundation of the apostles and prophets, with Christ Jesus himself as the *chief cornerstone*" (Eph. 2:20, italics added). This building, or temple, is the dwelling place of the Holy Spirit; it is comprised of all individuals in whom the Holy Spirit lives (1 Cor. 6:19ff). Hence, the building of God is not made with brick and mortar, but with people who are "living stones." An empty church building is not the church, even though it may be where the church meets. Those who attend are the dwelling place of God.

3. The church is *the bride of Christ.* Marriage illustrates Christ's relationship to the church (Eph. 5:25-27, 31-32; 2 Cor. 11:2; Rev. 19:7; 22:17). This metaphor powerfully displays *Christ's intense love* for His church and *His total commitment* to her.

To ask if one can become a Christian and not be joined to a body of believers, the building of God, or the bride of Christ would be tantamount to saying, "I'll be married, but not see the bride again or join in any of her activities. Maybe on Easter!" God's idea from the beginning was "setting the lonely in families," fulfilled in joining us into His covenant family. This is part of His plan for us when we trust His Son and are called "children of God" (Ps. 68:6; John 1:12). The biblical picture of the normal Christian life is to meet regularly together with other Christians.

A Close Look at the First Church

By reading the New Testament, we learn about the activities and membership requirements of the first church. The first meeting of the first church, as described in Acts 2:42, gives us a picture of its four prime activities.

> The New Testament church fulfilled God's promise to gather a people for His name through the Redeemer.

• The apostles and those who had been with Jesus *taught* them. All they had heard Jesus say and do, the apostles declared to the believers. The last week of Jesus' life was spent with the disciples, pouring out His heart with all the basics. He told them to make disciples of all nations teaching them "everything I have commanded you" (John 10–17; Matt. 28:20). For us, a church can only be founded on those basic biblical teachings.

• *Fellowship* was the second activity of the some 3,000 believers. This was not a routine visit to the local building called "church," followed by a quick exit and no contact for at least another week. There was mutual involvement, caring, studying the teaching, living as a close-knit community. This would be "oneness," as Jesus called it.

> ## THREE METAPHORS DESCRIBING THE CHURCH
>
> **The Body of Christ—**
> Christ is the Head, joining believers.
> **The Building of God—**
> A spiritual house of believers.
> **The Bride of Christ—**
> All believers have His divine love.

• *"The breaking of bread"* was their usual term for "the Lord's Supper," remembering Jesus' death. It was not a feast for the physically hungry, rather an event based on Jesus' words "do this in remembrance of me," in honor of His climactic death, the ultimate sacrifice of God for His church (Luke 22:19). Along with this, it was a time of inner examination, giving thanks and seeking purity of life congruent with obeying the Lord.

• *Prayer* was a common practice in the early church. The first meeting of the disciples as recorded in Acts 1:14 tells of them meeting to pray: "They all joined constantly in prayer." Acts also tells of other times of prayer: "Peter and John were going up to the temple at the time of prayer" (3:1); "[We] will give our attention to prayer and the ministry of the word" (6:4); "The church was earnestly praying to God for [Peter]" (12:5). Prayer was obviously a pattern for early believers.

Membership Requirements

Requirements for church membership focused on the basics.

1. *Belief in the Lord Jesus Christ* was the first ingredient (Acts 2:38). Faith in Christ, which normally included repentance for sin, was (and still is) the spiritual prerequisite to new life and membership in the body of Christ. When people asked Jesus the question, "What must we do to do the works God requires?" He answered, "The work of God is this: to *believe in the one he has sent*" (John 6:28-29, italics added).

2. *Baptism*, with repentance, was for everyone, "in the name of Jesus Christ for the forgiveness of your sins." Then believers received the promised follow-up of "the gift of the Holy Spirit" (Acts 2:38). From the practice of the Apostle John, Jesus Himself, Philip, and the Ethiopian, water baptism is implied as a practice of those who believe in God. Some earnest Christians believe that the "one baptism" (Eph. 4:5) is the baptism of the Holy Spirit, and that water baptism is not God's purpose for Christians today.

3. *Acting on revealed truth* was another membership requirement. Paul warned of false teachers arising within the church (Phil. 3:2), and Peter echoed the same solemn theme. Throughout the New Testament there is emphasis on doctrinal purity and holiness of life. Doctrinal or moral impurity were to be purged from the church (1 Cor. 5:7).

4. *Witnessing* was a visible characteristic of the church as a whole. Some had the special gift of evangelism. Their goal was the communication and preservation of the Gospel message to the immediate world and throughout the entire world (Matt. 28:19-20; Acts 1:8). Paul's letters placed little stress on evangelism, possibly because early believers were naturally and effectively evangelistic. He wrote to the Thessalonians: "The Lord's message rang out from you not only in Macedonia and Achaia—your faith in God has become known everywhere. Therefore we do not need to say anything about it" (1 Thess. 1:8). He called them "a model to all the believers" (v. 7).

5. *Serving* stood out as the normal function of church members as they met the physical and spiritual needs of both believers and unbelievers:

"As we have opportunity, let us do good to all people, especially to those who belong to the family of believers" (Gal. 6:10). Christ Himself was the example; He "went around doing good" (Acts 10:38).

As Leon Morris puts it, "During the history of the church there have been many variations from the New Testament pattern. Ministerial forms evolved in a variety of ways."[4] That there was some organization at the local level in New Testament times is evident. There were

- stated meetings (Acts 20:7)
- elected deacons (Acts 6:5-6)
- discipline of Christians (1 Cor. 5:13)
- letters of commendation (Acts 18:27)
- lists of widows for support (1 Tim. 5:9)

God gave spiritual gifts to the church to prepare God's people for *works of service*, "so that the body of Christ may be built up" (Eph. 4:11-12). There is no clear distinction between clergy and laity, either in terms of church government or spiritual ministry.

Periods of Ministry

T.C. Hammond outlines the three periods in the development of the organizational structure of the New Testament ministry.

- *The first period included the following:*
  —Jesus' ministry with the seventy whom He commissioned,
  —the apostolic ministry of those given leadership after Pentecost, and
  —the ministry of deacons, elders, and bishops. (The three pastoral epistles give the principles and qualifications for the ministry in 1–2 Timothy and Titus.)

- *The transitional period.* During most of the lifetime of the apostles, the New Testament had been circulated to the various Christian communities. The aim was to ensure the local community had received the New Testament revelation of Christ direct from the Spirit of God. There was no evidence of an unending succession of apostles and prophets (Eph. 2:20; 3:5; 4:11).

- *The permanent ministry.* A *bishop, or elder*, taught spiritual truth and

exercised rule and discipline in the local church. "Remember your leaders, who spoke the word of God to you. Consider the outcome of their
way of life and imitate their faith" (Heb. 13:7; see also 1 Tim. 5:17).[5]
Deacons also helped administer the business of a church (Acts 6:1-6;
1 Tim. 3:8-12), though it is clear there are spiritual overtones to their
activity.

In many denominations and sects throughout church history, the
views of the ministry fall generally into one of three groups: the episcopal, the presbyterial, or the congregational.[6] These terms, as here used,
refer to *systems of church government* rather than to denominations.

Episcopalianism

The church is *governed by bishops* in the episcopalian system, and they
hold the major authority. Also, there are presbyters (or priests) and deacons under him/her. Only bishops have power to ordain. They trace their
office back centuries to the apostles, hence the term used is "apostolic
succession." The Roman Catholic, Orthodox, Anglican, Episcopal,
Methodist, and some Lutheran churches have the episcopal form of government.

This system is actually not found in the New Testament. Those who
hold to this type of church government, however, feel that it was a natural development in the second-century church. They see, in the work of
some New Testament figures, a transition between the itinerant ministry
of the apostles and the more settled ministry of the later bishops.

For example, Timothy and Titus had a good deal of authority over a
number of churches, yet lacked the wide apostolic authority of Paul.
James of Jerusalem is, some believe, an example of an apostle who had a
localized ministry but was more like a bishop than like Paul. The development of episcopacy is traced through the early church fathers. By the
second century, the episcopal system predominated throughout the
whole church.

Presbyterianism

The church is *governed by elders* in presbyterianism. Presbyterians recognize that in the New Testament the terms *elder* and *bishop* are used inter-
changeably, are considered *equal to each other*, and are clearly very important in the group's ministry. In each local church, it would seem, a num-

ber of elders formed a kind of committee to handle church affairs. In New Testament times they acted with the apostles (Acts 15) and when the apostles finally passed from the scene, elders became the leading officers.

The members of the local congregation also appear to have had a voice in the selection of those who would minister to them. They chose the seven deacons (Acts 6:1-6) and apparently had a hand in setting aside Paul and Barnabas for missionary work (Acts 12:1-3). The congregation also had the right to take part (through their representatives) in the government of a church. The unity of the church was maintained through a graduated series of church courts. "This carefully devised system of graded church courts were legislative, executive, and judicial—not merely advisory—powers."[7]

Presbyterians usually make a distinction between teaching and ruling elders (1 Tim. 5:17). The *teaching elder* is the principal minister, ordained by the "laying on of the hands" of other elders. This is, in the presbyterial view, ordination to the church worldwide, not to some small part of it.

Ruling elders are chosen by the congregation and admitted to their office by ordination. They may not preach, baptize, or administer Communion, but they assist in the government of the church and in the exercise of discipline. They also have responsibility for the financial affairs of the church.

The word *ordination* is not used anywhere in the New Testament. The RSV translates the word as "appoint" (Acts 14:23). Both Mark (13:14) and Luke (6:13-16) record Jesus' calling those He wanted to be with Him, that is "the twelve." He designated them as apostles, meaning "messenger" or "one sent with a special commission." It is significant that both Mark and Luke tell of Jesus spending the previous night in prayer. Matthias was simply "enrolled" as a replacement apostle for Judas (Acts 1:26, RSV).

When the need arose for some to care for the needy in the church, the twelve apostles appointed "the Seven," as they came to be known, for this work. With prayer and laying on of hands these men were appointed. The actions of laying on of hands and prayer were frequently used in ways other than to appoint someone to a work, and were even practiced in the Old Testament. It is difficult to see, however, in this kind of event a prototype ordination.[8]

Congregationalism

The *local congregation is autonomous* in the congregational form of church government. Every group whose emphasis is on the *autonomy of the each congregation* would be included here. Such groups include Baptists, the Evangelical Free Church, the Open Brethren, Christians (Disciples), and some Bible and other independent churches. Followers of this polity hold that no one man or group of men should exercise authority over a local congregation of Christ's church.

With some exceptions, these churches have two types of ministers—*pastors* and *deacons*. Pastors have oversight of the congregation. They are usually ordained or set apart in a service attended by representatives of other similar congregations. Deacons (or, sometimes, elders) are generally assigned the responsibility of watching over the spiritual and material needs of the local congregation. Congregationalists, as most other Protestants, deny that ordination imparts special grace to a man.

Two basic ideas are behind the congregational view of the ministry, and they have biblical precedent. One is that *Christ is the Head of His church*, in living, vital contact with it. It is not two or three officials, but two or three *believers*, gathered together in His name, in whose midst Christ promises to be (Matt. 18:20).

The second basic idea is the *priesthood of all believers*, common to most other Protestants as well. Strictly speaking, there are no laymen in the church. All believers are priests (1 Peter 2:9)—that is, representatives of God to witness and minister to men in His name and power.

Almost all churches fit into one of the above three groupings so far as polity is concerned.

According to biblical teaching each Christian is also a *saint*, implying a person is holy through Christ's new life. Since human righteousness falls far short of God's personal holiness, a *"bestowed" or given righteousness* is ours when we wholeheartedly believe in Christ's death. This happens at the new birth or salvation. We do not achieve sainthood by our own achievements or greatness "but . . . through . . . righteousness that comes from God and is by faith" (Phil. 3:9).

Church Ordinances

There are numerous differences of opinion about the number and nature of *ordinances* or *sacraments* in the church. Ordinances are outward rites that signify or represent spiritual grace or blessing. The Roman Catholic church has seven sacraments: baptism, the Lord's Supper, confirmation, penance, orders, matrimony, and extreme unction. Protestants maintain, however, that Scripture recognizes only two ordinances—baptism and the Lord's Supper.

Generally, Roman Catholics teach that objective merit or grace is conferred by the sacraments. By contrast to this seeming mechanical view, most Protestants emphasize faith and the working of God directly in each believer.

The meaning of *baptism* is perhaps most fully explained in Romans 6:1-4 (though some Christians insist that this chapter does not have baptism with water in view). Baptism has been called "an outward sign of an inward grace," a declaration and public identification with Christ in His death, burial, and resurrection.

Protestants are divided on the issue of baptism: should it be only adults who make a profession of faith in Christ, or should infants also be baptized? Episcopalians, Presbyterians, Lutherans, Methodists, and certain others practice infant baptism, whereas Baptists, Disciples, and a great number of independent churches hold to baptism following belief. (Those who are baptized as infants often later make some public declaration of faith, usually as they enter into a personal commitment to Christ).

For *the Lord's Supper* most Christians agree on their obligation to observe the Lord's request, "Do this in remembrance of me." The Lord's Supper was to be a memorial and a "showing forth," or declaration, of His death till He returns (1 Cor. 11:23-26).

Roman Catholics teach that in the Lord's Supper the bread and wine become the *actual* body and blood of our Lord, though their appearance remains the same. This view is called *transubstantiation*. This view assumes that the body and blood of Christ are offered every time the mass is observed. Scripture, however, emphatically contradicts such ideas. Christ's death on the cross was a complete and fully effective sacrifice, and He died once for all (Heb. 10:10; 7:27; 9:12).

Lutherans believe in *consubstantiation*. In this view, Christ is present with the unchanged substance of the bread.

Most Protestants, however, believe either that the elements are a *symbolic memorial* or that by faith the believer, in the Communion, enters into a special spiritual union with his Savior, Jesus Christ.

Though participation in neither of these ordinances alone makes a person a Christian, every true believer should want to show his devotion to Christ by giving public witness in baptism and by remembering Him in the Lord's Supper.

No "Lone-wolf" Christians

There is no such thing as a *"lone-wolf" Christian*. Each genuine Christian, regardless of denomination, is spiritually one with every other believer. All are in the church universal. We are united in Christ, who is our life.

When Christians are alive to Jesus Christ, they are like coals in a fire—they keep the flame alive as they stay connected. Left alone, coals die out. When Christians separate and become lone wolves they too can grow cold in their own hearts.

If we are obedient to our Lord, we will identify with and join other believers for worship and service. In so doing, we not only contribute our own unique gifts to the fellowship to be used by God to help bless others, but we are also blessed.

10

Things to Come

O ne of the most fascinating features of the Bible is that it tells what is ahead for our world. Both Old and New Testaments contend that history is moving to a climax and that the sovereign God is in control. Helmut Thielicke, in his book *The Waiting Father*, sums up this truth in a magnificent way:

> When the drama of history is over, Jesus Christ will stand alone upon the stage. All the great figures of history—Pharaoh, Alexander the Great, Charlemagne, Churchill, Stalin, Johnson, Mao Tse-tung—will realize they have been bit actors in a drama produced by Another.[1]

Throughout the Old Testament, the prophets looked forward to "the Day of the Lord" and to the intervention of God in reclaiming the world and bringing the resolution of evil. For those who worship God it will be a day of glorious hope; for those who serve evil and turn from God, final judgment will come.

The prophets envisioned a picture of security for God's people—a time when nations would serve the God of Israel and a time when the law would be written on their hearts. The prophecies centered on the coming of the Messiah who would rule the world in righteousness (Isa. 2:2, 4; 65:21ff; Jer. 31:31ff).

Two terms describe this coming Deliverer in the Old Testament prophecies.

• The first coming pictures the Messiah as *the Suffering Servant*. The Prophet Isaiah (Isa. 53) lists *fifteen specific details* that were fulfilled exactly in Jesus' death. Verses 3-12 speak of His suffering, rejection by His people, silence before His accusers, taking our sins on Himself, being treated unjustly, burial with rich people, and His resurrection from the dead. It has been said that the odds of just *eight* prophecies fulfilled in exact detail are one in 10^{17}. This *first coming* of Christ in Bethlehem, as the Suffering Servant, answered the hope of God's people for a Messiah who brings forgiveness and redemption for His people.

> **Two terms in the Old Testament describe the coming Deliverer:**
>
> **The Suffering Servant**—already meticulously fulfilled (Zech. 9:9).
>
> **The Reigning King—** "He will proclaim peace to the nations. His rule will extend from sea to sea" (Zech. 9:10).

Through the cross and the Resurrection, Satan has been judicially conquered so that "by his death he might destroy him who holds the power of death—that is, the devil" (Heb. 2:14). Satan, however, is temporarily "the god of this age" (2 Cor. 4:4), and he actively continues to oppose Christ and His church.

• At the second coming of Christ, He will come as *the Reigning King:* "For to us a child is born, to us a son is given, and the government will be on his shoulders. And he will be called Wonderful Counselor, Mighty God, Everlasting Father, Prince of Peace. Of the increase of his government and peace there will be no end" (Isa. 9:6-7).

The final rule of God in Christ will be consummated in this future second coming. The prophets used both terms, *the Suffering Servant* and *the*

Reigning King. They "searched intently and with the greatest care" the details of the Redeemer's coming without fully comprehending how and when their prophecies would be fulfilled (1 Peter 1:10-12). Zechariah most explicitly told of both aspects, saying the King would arrive "righteous and having salvation, gentle and riding on a donkey. . . . He will proclaim peace to the nations. His rule will extend from sea to sea and from the River to the ends of the earth" (Zech. 9:9-10).

Jesus Is Coming!

The glorious and incontestable fact that *Jesus is coming the second time* is the Christian's firm hope; however, the revealed details take some thought and study. Jesus' own description of His "Second Coming" cannot be equaled. "I will come back and take you to be with me that you also may be where I am" (John 14:3). "Immediately after the distress of those days . . . the sign of the Son of Man will appear in the sky. . . . They will see the Son of Man coming on the clouds of the sky, with power and great glory" (Matt. 24:29-30).

At His ascension into heaven while the disciples stared heavenward, two men dressed in white stood beside them and said: "Men of Galilee

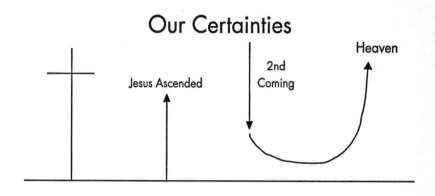

Our Certainties

Jesus Ascended

2nd Coming

Heaven

1 John 3:3
Everyone who has this hope
in him purifies himself as He is pure

2 Cor. 5:8
Away from the body;
at home with the Lord

Phil. 1:23
To depart and be with Christ
is far better

. . . why do you stand here looking into the sky? This same Jesus, who has been taken from you into heaven, will come back in the same way you have seen him go into heaven" (Acts 1:10-11). Paul also emphasized it: "For the Lord himself will come down from heaven, with a loud command, with the voice of the archangel and with the trumpet call of God, and the dead in Christ will rise first" (1 Thess. 4:16).

The second coming of Christ is the great expectation of the church. As Christians we should, with Paul, love to look for that "blessed hope [and] the glorious appearing of our great God and our Savior, Jesus Christ" (Titus 2:13). His coming is an incentive for holy living: "And now, dear children, continue in him, so that when he appears we may be confident and unashamed before him at his coming" (1 John 2:28). "Everyone who has this hope in him purifies himself, just as he is pure" (1 John 3:3).

Neither the prophets nor the apostles mention the return of Christ for speculative purposes, but always as a motive for practical daily holiness. We could summarize this doctrine with Peter's words: "What kind of people ought you to be? You ought to live holy and godly lives" (2 Peter 3:11).

The Tribulation

Some events prior to the second coming of Christ are included by the New Testament writers although they also saw the Second Coming as immanent, the next event. Jesus gave a preview of some of these "end times" in His words on the Mount of Olives (Matt. 24; Mark 13; Luke 21).

The Tribulation is one inevitable thing that will precede Jesus' coming (Rev. 7:14). Satan's longtime and persistent opposition to God's work will accelerate to an extreme and be seen by all.

Looming large at this time is the appearance of a being called "Antichrist," heightening *opposition* to God and Christ. Before this person appears, the "spirit of antichrist" will be seen. In fact, his presence was noted already in apostolic times: "Dear children, this is the last hour; and as you have heard that the antichrist is coming, even now *many* antichrists have come. This is how we know it is the last hour" (1 John 2:18, italics added). Of this Antichrist John asked, "Who is the liar? It is the man who denies that Jesus is the Christ. Such a man is the antichrist—he *denies the Father and the Son*" (1 John 2:22, italics added).

Though there is considerable difference of opinion among Bible scholars, some feel the description given in Daniel 11:37 and 2 Thessalonians 2:4 refers to this same Antichrist. One thing stands out, these verses, along with a description of "the beast" in Revelation 13:3, 13, 16-17, present several striking similarities.

Satan will empower the Antichrist to act supernaturally with a view to deceiving and persuading men. He may act as an ecclesiastical leader, *manipulate religion* for his own ends, and claim the worship due God. He will also *demand political allegiance* and *exercise economic pressure* to force compliance (Rev. 13:16-17). Those who try to oppose him will face trouble so great that unless God shortened the days no one would survive (Matt. 24:21-22).

Bible scholars give three differing views concerning whether believers will go through the final great Tribulation or be taken to be with Christ before it.

1. The *pretribulation view* holds that Christ will return for His church *before* the Great Tribulation, thus allowing believers to escape the worst horror. Now called "the Rapture," this view cites Revelation 7:14: "These are they who have come out of the great tribulation."

This Tribulation appears to coincide with the seventieth "seven" mentioned in Daniel's prophecy: "And he [the prince that is to come, or Antichrist] will confirm a covenant with many [with Israel] for one 'seven.' In the middle of the 'seven' he will put an end to sacrifice and offering [in the temple at Jerusalem]. And on a wing of the temple he will set up an abomination that causes desolation, until the end that is decreed is poured out on him" (Dan. 9:27).

By comparing the whole prophecy (Dan. 9) with parallel passages, these "sevens" are "sevens" of *years*, not *days*, according to pretribulation interpretation. Thus, the Tribulation will be a literal seven-year period, ruled by Antichrist, just before his final defeat by Christ.

2. The *midtribulation view* holds that the Rapture will take place in the *middle* of the seventieth "seven," three-and-a-half years after its beginning.

3. The *posttribulation view* interprets Christ's coming *for* His saints and His revelation (coming *with* His saints) are *one and the same event*, occurring just *after* the Tribulation.

Is Anything Yet to Happen Before Christ Returns?

Those holding the *pretribulation* view feel there is nothing to prevent the Rapture from happening at "any moment." This "perhaps today" awareness encourages many Christians to live each day in the light of their Lord's imminent return. Most of those having *midtribulation* or *posttribulation* convictions believe, of course, that certain events (primarily the Tribulation, or the first half of it) must take place before Christ comes again to earth.

Despite the differing views, each of us Christians can assuredly look forward to the indescribable glory and deliverance that will be ours when He comes. This is our "blessed hope"—to see Jesus Christ come back as the disciples saw Him go into heaven.

The Millennium

Another related and important question has to do with the *period of 1,000 years* (alluded to as the Millennium by scholars) foretold in Scripture, specifically by John in Revelation 20:1-10. Three stages characterize this period, beginning with Christ reigning in peace as told in verses 1-4. Satan is bound and can no longer deceive people for this 1,000-year period. It is an idyllic millennium.

• *Premillennialists* believe Christ will come to reign for a literal 1,000 years on earth. Finally, Satan will be bound and can no longer deceive the nations. The Millennium, then, is an extension and visible expression of Christ's reigning in the hearts of His people on earth and in heaven. Some see it as a fulfillment of God's promises to Israel, involving the restoration of the Jews to their homeland as a nation and the reestablishment of a literal throne, king, temple, and sacrificial system.

The second period John shows us in Revelation 20:4-6. During this time, the martyrs "who had been beheaded because of their testimony for Jesus and because of the word of God . . . came to life and reigned with Christ a thousand years" (v. 4).

In Revelation 20:7-10, the third period sees the end of the 1,000 years. Satan is released and, with his cohorts, seeks to organize nations against God. But quickly he and those with him are summarily overcome by God and thrown into the lake of fire for eternal torment.

• *Amillennialists* believe the idea of a literal Millennium cannot be harmonized with the whole of biblical eschatology. They view the Millennium as only a symbol of the ideal church, not a literal reign. The Millennium, then, will be a visible expression of Christ's reign in the hearts of His people or the fulfillment of God's promises to Israel, involving the restoration of the Jews to their homeland.

• *Postmillennialists* see the influence of the Gospel as an increasing force for good that eventually leads to righteousness and peace on earth. The missionary task of the church, they claim, includes the ultimate Christianization of society.[2]

Whatever points of view expositors take on the Tribulation, the Rapture, and the Millennium, it is thrilling to realize we all agree on the great, glorious, and incontestable fact that *Jesus is coming again.*

Resurrection: Believers and Unbelievers

Extraordinary and momentous events will take place at the coming of Christ. The resurrection of the believing dead will occur, and we [believers] who are still alive will be changed and "caught up together with them in the clouds to meet the Lord in the air" (1 Thess. 4:17; see also 1 Cor. 15:52). The resurrection of the dead is emphasized in the New Testament, but it is taught throughout Scripture. Job said: "I know that my Redeemer lives, and that in the end he will stand upon the earth. And after my skin has been destroyed, yet *in my flesh* I will see God; I myself will see him with my own eyes—I, and not another" (Job 19:25-27, italics added).

David anticipated this resurrection (Ps. 16:9), and Daniel mentioned it (Dan. 12:1-3). Jesus taught it repeatedly and emphasized that it will include *all* people: "A time is coming when all who are in their graves will hear his voice and come out—those who have done good will rise to live, and those who have done evil will rise to be condemned (John 5:28-29). That the resurrection is a physical rather than a merely spiritual event is evidenced by the resurrection of Lazarus (John 11:44) and by that of our Lord Himself (Luke 24:39).

The resurrection of the body is part of our total redemption (Rom. 8:23). A Christian should not long to be delivered from the body, with all of its weaknesses and problems, but for the body's *redemption.* Paul refers to our resurrection bodies as "clothed with our heavenly dwelling,"

or "an eternal house" not built by human hands. (2 Cor. 5:1, 4). Our resurrection bodies will not be identical to the ones we have now, but they
will be closely related to them. The disciples, for example, recognized
Jesus by the scars in His hands and side (John 20:27).

Believers will be resurrected at the coming of Christ (1 Thess. 4:16).
This will be the first resurrection (see John 5:28-29), of which Paul wanted to be part (Phil. 3:11). It is literally the resurrection "out of the dead."
That is, the righteous will be raised from among the wicked.

There is indication of a *time lapse* between the resurrection of believers to glory and the resurrection of unbelievers to judgment. Though we
cannot be dogmatic as to the exact length of this interval, *at least 1,000*
years will separate the two resurrections. Here it seems appropriate to
look again at the complete account from Revelation: "I saw the souls of
those who had been beheaded because of their testimony for Jesus and
because of the word of God. They had not worshiped the beast or his
image and had not received his mark on their foreheads or their hands.
They came to life and reigned with Christ a thousand years. (The rest of
the dead did not come to life until the thousand years were ended.) This
is the first resurrection. Blessed and holy are those who have part in the
first resurrection. The second death has no power over them, but they
will be priests of God and of Christ and will reign with him for a thousand years" (Rev. 20:4-6).

Where Are the Dead Before the Resurrection?

What about the condition of the dead believers before they are resurrected? It seems clear that the soul is without a body and that believers
are in a condition of conscious joy. Paul was willing "to be away from the
body and at home with the Lord" (2 Cor. 5:8). He said, referring to
death, that he preferred "to depart and be with Christ, which is better by
far" (Phil. 1:23). Dead believers are at rest: "Blessed are the dead who die
in the Lord. . . . They will rest from their labor" (Rev. 14:13).

The Scriptures affirm the conscious existence of both the wicked and
the righteous after death and before their resurrections, but give few
details. Unbelievers, however, await the resurrection in a state of suffering (Luke 16:24).

Death is frequently described in the Bible as sleep. In the Old
Testament the term *sleep* is applied to *all* the dead, but in the New
Testament it applies mostly to the *righteous* dead. Paul used the word only

of believers. This term does not apply to the soul or spirit; it does not imply total unconsciousness until the resurrection. It rather implies unconsciousness with reference to *earthly life*, for which consciousness of the body is necessary. The dead are "asleep" so far as this world is concerned, but this in no way implies that they are asleep or unconscious to the other world or that their spirits are totally unconscious.

"Soul-sleep" is nowhere taught in Scripture. Passages quoted to prove this doctrine refer primarily to bodily or physical life. All that we have said about the state of the righteous dead bears this out.

The consciousness of the unrighteous dead is also clearly taught. They are in prison (1 Peter 3:19), which would be unnecessary if they were unconscious. The story of the rich man and Lazarus (Luke 16:19-31), whatever else it may or may not teach, shows that the unrighteous dead experience conscious suffering and punishment.

Evidence of Purgatory

The passages cited regarding what happens to people after they die give no evidence of purgatory. A person dies either as one who has been redeemed or as one who is under judgment. After death there is no passing over from one condition to the other. Final judgment or redemption simply settles what has already begun at the time of death.

The Bible says more about the condition of the dead than about their location. In the Old Testament the souls of all the dead are spoken of as going to *sheol*, which is translated *grave*, *hell*, or *pit*: "You will not abandon me to the grave, nor will you let your Holy One see decay" (Ps. 16:10). Sheol is a place of sorrow. "The snares of death [sheol] confronted me," said David (2 Sam. 22:6). *Hades*, translated *hell* and *grave*, is the New Testament equivalent of sheol. Other New Testament terms for the intermediate state include *paradise* (Luke 23:43) and *Abraham's side* (16:22).

The Judgments

But the intermediate state will be succeeded at last by the final judgment, toward which all history is heading. God is the Ruler of all men, the Lawgiver, and the final Judge. Sometimes the Bible mentions God (the Father) as judge: "God, the judge of all" (Heb. 12:23); and sometimes it mentions Christ as judge: " Christ Jesus, who will judge the living and the dead" (2 Tim. 4:1). The relationship of the Father and the Son in judgment is made clear: "He [God, the Father] has set a day when he will judge the world with justice by the man [Christ] he has appointed. He has given proof of this to all men by raising him from the dead" (Acts 17:31).

God is judging men and nations continually, but there will be a final judgment that all previous judgments foreshadow. It will be an extension of past and present judgments. An unbeliever "stands *condemned* already because he has not believed in the name of God's one and only Son" (John 3:18, italics added).

The purpose of final judgment will not be to *ascertain* the quality of an individual's character, but rather to *disclose* his character and to assign him to the eternal place corresponding to what he is because of his trust or lack of trust in God.

Several future judgments are mentioned in Scripture. The judgment of the living nations (Matt. 25:31-46), according to premillennialists, will take place at the return of Christ with His saints. It will lead to the setting up of the millennial kingdom.

Believers will be judged, but not with unbelievers: "We must all appear before the judgment seat of Christ, that each one may receive what is due him for the things done while in the body, whether good or bad" (2 Cor. 5:10).

Plainly stated, this judgment does not decide a believer's salvation, but it appraises his works. A Christian, in this judgment, can suffer loss of reward. "This is a judgment, not for destiny, but for adjustment, for reward or loss, according to our works, for position in the kingdom: every man according as his work shall be," writes William Evans.[3]

The final judgment of the unsaved will be at the Great White Throne of God. John describes it: "I saw a great white throne and him who was seated on it. Earth and sky fled from his presence, and there was no place for them. And I saw the dead, great and small, standing before the throne, and books were opened. Another book was opened, which is the book of life. The dead were judged according to what they had done as recorded in the books"

> To be with Christ for believers is a condition of conscious joy: "I desire to depart and be with Christ, which is better by far" (Phil. 1:23).

(Rev. 20:11-12).

The final judgment of Satan will occur just before that of the Great White Throne: "The devil, who deceived them [men], was thrown into the lake of burning sulfur" (Rev. 20:10). Presumably Satan's angels will be judged at the same time, for Jesus spoke of "eternal fire prepared for the devil *and his angels*" (Matt. 25:41, italics added).

Hell

The final destiny of the wicked is hell. This awesome place is described in various ways. It is a place or state of everlasting fire (Mark 9:43; Matt. 25:41). It is spoken of as a lake of burning sulfur (Rev. 20:10).

Hell is conceived of as outer darkness (Matt. 8:12). It is described as a place of eternal torment and punishment (Rev. 14:10-11). If figurative language is involved, it is obviously symbolic of something so awful no one in his right mind could be indifferent to avoiding it. A.H. Strong describes hell this way: "the loss of all good, whether physical or spiritual, and the misery of an evil conscience banished from God and the society of the holy and dwelling under God's positive curse forever."[4]

Nowhere in Scripture is there any trace of the idea that hell is a kind of "Jolly Boys' Club," absence from which would cause us to miss our friends. This flippant notion is Satan's lie. Hell is "the blackest darkness forever" (Jude 13)—utter aloneness. C.S. Lewis defined hell as "nothing but yourself for all eternity!"[5] This is not the whole truth about hell, but it describes one of its most awful aspects.

A good resting place for our understanding about hell is God's holiness. Could He let Hitler go without paying for the consequences of his sin? God's character revolts at *any sin*, not only the gross ones.

There is no biblical evidence for believing in the final restoration of the lost or in the universal salvation of all men. Perhaps the clearest disproof of these notions, as well as of final annihilation, is the fact that the same word, *eternal*, is used to describe both punishment and life: "Then they will go away to *eternal* punishment, but the righteous to *eternal* life" (Matt. 25:46, italics added). However we may try to qualify the word so that it means "age-long" rather than "everlasting," we must apply the same qualification to the destinies of the righteous and the wicked. We cannot, consistently, deny eternal punishment without also denying eternal life. And "eternal life" is *everlasting* life. *Eternal* certainly means "everlasting" when it is applied to God. Why should it mean anything else when it modifies "punishment"?

There are, however, *degrees* of punishment in hell and of reward in heaven. Christians, at "the judgment seat of Christ" in heaven, will suffer loss of reward because their works of "wood, hay, or straw" will not stand the test of fire (1 Cor. 3:12-15). Simply expressed, their capacity for enjoyment, though unlimited in duration, will be less than that of other Christians.

God, in His love, has done everything necessary to redeem man. (Remember His admonition to Adam and Eve: "Don't eat!") His justice requires that He punish sin, but His love provides salvation freely for all who will accept it. Those in hell are there because they refused or ignored God's love; they are solely responsible for their condition. The realization of this truth will surely be one of the most painful experiences of perdition.

Heaven

The final destiny of the righteous is heaven. Heaven is most simply defined as where God is. It is a place of rest (Heb. 4:9), of glory (2 Cor. 4:17), of purity (Rev. 21:27), of worship (Rev. 19:1), of fellowship with others (Heb. 12:23), and of being with God (Rev. 21:3). "He will wipe every tear from their eyes. There will be no more death or mourning or crying or pain, for the old order of things has passed away" (Rev. 21:4).

Believers may receive one or more crowns—the crown of life (James 1:12), the crown of glory (1 Peter 5:4), and the crown of righteousness (2 Tim. 4:8). Those who have been won for Christ through our witness become our crown of rejoicing (I Thess. 2:19). Through all of this, the center of heaven will be God Himself, the Lord of heaven. Those around His throne are pictured as being in such awe that they cast their crowns before Him, and say, "You are worthy, our Lord and God" (Rev. 4:11).

Everything in heaven will be new: "The earth and everything in it will be laid bare. . . . But . . . we are looking forward to a new heaven and a new earth, the home of righteousness" (2 Peter 3:10, 13). John reports: "I saw a new heaven and a new earth, for the first heaven and the first earth had passed away, and there was no longer any sea. I saw the Holy City, the new Jerusalem, coming down out of heaven from God" (Rev. 21:1-2).

God's kingdom will be established when "at the name of Jesus every knee [shall] bow . . . and every tongue confess that Jesus Christ is Lord, to the glory of God the Father" (Phil. 2:10-11). The kingdoms of this world shall be the kingdoms of our Lord, and He shall reign forever and ever. *His will* be done on earth as it is done in heaven. Imagine this sight: "[I saw] someone 'like a son of man,' dressed in a robe reaching down to his feet. . . . His head and hair were white like wool, as white as snow, and his eyes were like blazing fire. His feet were like bronze glowing in a furnace, and his voice was like the sound of rushing waters" (Rev. 1:13-15).

This is our hope—to see with our resurrection eyes the Lord Jesus, a sight that outstrips our comprehension.

Heaven could never be the boring experience of strumming a harp on a cloud, as some facetiously characterize it. It will be the most dynamic, expanding, exhilarating experience conceivable. Our problem now is that, with our finite minds, we cannot imagine it. In the classic words of John Newton:

> *When we've been there ten thousand years*
> *Bright shining as the sun,*
> *We've no less days to sing God's praise*
> *Than when we first begun.*

Endnotes

Chapter 1

1. Andrew E. Hill and John H. Walton, *A Survey of the Old Testament* (Grand Rapids: Zondervan, 1991), p. 437.

2. Ibid., p. 16.

3. B.B. Warfield, *The Inspiration and Authority of the Bible* (New York: Oxford University Press, 1927), p. 299.

4. Hill and Walton, *A Survey*, p. 435.

5. J.N. Birdsell, "Canon of the New Testament," in *New Bible Dictionary (NBD)* (Grand Rapids: Wm. B. Eerdmans Publishing Co., 1962), p. 194.

6. A.R. Millard, *Treasures from Bible Times* (Oxford, England: Lion Publishing, 1985), p. 14.

7. "Rocker Boy George," *Servant Magazine* (winter 1996), p. 9.

8. Martyn Lloyd-Jones, *Joy Unspeakable* (Wheaton, Ill.: Harold Shaw Publishers, 1984), p. 106.

Chapter 2

1. C.S. Lewis, *Miracles* (New York: Macmillan Co., 1947), p. 28.

2. Hugh Ross, *Fingerprint of God* (Orange, Calif.: Promise Publishing Co., 1991), p. 180.

3. A.H. Strong, *Systematic Theology* (Philadelphia: Judson Press, 1907), p. 255.

4. Hammond, *In Understanding Be Men* (Downers Grove, Ill.: InterVarsity Press, 1968), p. 44.

5. R.A. Finlayson, "Holiness," *NBD*, p. 530.

6. Ibid., p. 530.

7. R.A. Finlayson, "Trinity," *NBD*, p. 1298.

8. Ibid., p. 1298.

9. Ibid., p. 1300.

10. Hammond, *In Understanding*, p. 54.

11. Finlayson, "Trinity," *NBD*, p. 1300.

12. Hammond, *In Understanding*, p. 66.

13. Ibid., p. 56.

14. Ross, *Fingerprint of God*, p. 180.

15. J.I. Packer, *Evangelism and the Sovereignty of God* (Downers Grove, Ill.: InterVarsity Press, 1961), pp. 18-19.

Chapter 3

1. Oswald Chambers, *Living Quotations* (New York: Harper & Row, 1974), No. 1709.

2. Strong, *Theology*, p. 676.

3. Ibid., p. 673.

4. Hammond, *In Understanding*, p. 101.

5. R.A. Finlayson, *The Story of Theology* (Downers Grove, Ill.: InterVarsity Press, 1963), pp. 24-25.

Chapter 4

1. Leon Morris, "Atonement," *NBD*, p. 108.

2. Leon Morris, "Propitiation," *NBD*, p. 1046.

3. Strong, *Theology*, p. 740.

4. Finlayson, *Theology*, p. 381

5. Strong, *Theology*, p. 766.

6. James Denney, *The Death of Christ* (Downers Grove, Ill.: InterVarsity Press, 1964), p. 3.

7. Hammond, *In Understanding*, p. 122.

8. Robert J. Little, *Here's Your Answer* (Chicago: Moody Press, 1967), p. 206.

Chapter 5

1. John Stott, *Basic Christianity* (Downers Grove, Ill. : InterVarsity Press, 1975), p. 71.

2. Derek Williams, "Heart," in *New Concise Bible Dictionary* (Downers Grove, Ill.: InterVasity Press, 1989), p. 214

3. Hammond, *In Understanding*, p. 71.

4. D.M. Edwards, "Image," in *International Standard Bible Encyclopedia (ISBE)* (Grand Rapids: Wm. B. Eerdmans Publishing Co., 1939), p. 1450.

5. Hammond, *In Understanding*, p. 77.

6. John Murray, "Sin," *NBD*, p. 1190.

Chapter 6

1. Walters, "Holy Spirit," *NBD*, p. 531ff.
2. Mullins, "Holy Spirit," *ISBE*, p. 1409.
3. Derek Williams, "Holy Spirit," in *New Concise Bible Dictionary* (Downers Grove, Ill.: InterVarsity Press), p. 528.
4. William Barclay, *The Gospel of John* (Philadelphia: The Westminster Press, 1956), pp. 225-226.
5. Romans 12:3-8; 1 Corinthians 12:8-11, 28-30; Ephesians 4:11-12.

Chapter 7

1. Leon Morris, "Faith," *NBD*, p. 413.
2. Strong, *Theology*, p. 809.
3. J.I. Packer, "Election," *NBD*, p. 360.
4. Charles Simeon, *Expository Outlines on the Whole Bible* (Grand Rapids: Zondervan, reprinted 1956), vol. I, pp. xvii-xviii.

Chapter 8

1. Robert Little, "Here's Your Answer," *Moody Monthly*, 1968, 192.
2. Billy Graham, "Angels All Around," *Decision Magazine*, December 1996, vol. 37.

Chapter 9

1. D.W.B. Robinson, "Church," *NBD*, pp. 228-229
2. Strong, *Theology*, p. 887.
3. Ibid., p. 890.
4. Leon Morris, *Ministers of God* (Downers Grove, Ill.: InterVarsity Press, 1969), p. 91.
5. Hammond, *In Understanding*, p. 162ff.
6. Morris, *Ministers of God*, p. 92ff.
7. John Dall, *Encyclopedia of Religion and Ethics* (Edinburgh: T. & T. Clark, 1918), p. 264.
8. Derek Williams, "Ordination," in *New Concise Bible Dictionary* (Downers Grove, Ill.: InterVarsity Press), p. 398.

Chapter 10

1. Helmut Thielicke, *The Waiting Father* (New York: Harper, 1959).

2. George E. Ladd, "Eschatology," *NBD*, p. 390.

3. William Evans, *The Great Doctrines of the Bible* (Chicago: Moody Press, 1949), p. 254.

4. Strong, *Theology*, p. 1034.

5. C.S. Lewis, *The Letters of C.S. Lewis to Arthur Greeves*, ed. Walter Hooper (New York: Macmillan Co., 1979), p. 508.

Study Questions

Chapter 1
Theme: The Bible is the written Word of God.

1. Why do we all need the Bible, especially in today's society?

2. Why was the Bible written?

3. When people say, "The Bible is inspired," what do they mean?

4. How would you explain the phrase "canon of Scripture?"

5. Looking back, what was your primary source of religious belief in your growing-up years? If you now have a new primary source, what caused the shift?

6. What are some questions you could ask yourself when you are trying to interpret a passage of Scripture?

7. How would you respond to this statement: "The Bible is not scientifically accurate?"

8. Explain the statement: "We do not prove the Bible by archaeology."

9. What do a television set and the Word of God have in common?

10. How can you feed on the Word of God? (Think of specific actions.)

> *Belief in the Bible doesn't make it true; belief enables me to enter into what is already true.*

Chapter 2

Theme: What we believe about God influences our actions, attitudes, and view of the world.

1. Explain this statement: "Our personal concept of God—when we pray, for instance—is worthless unless it is coherent and coincides with His self-revelation."

2. One of the ways God has revealed Himself to us is through His natural attributes. List and explain four of these attributes.

3. *God is personal.* What does that statement mean? How have you experienced the truth of that statement?

4. List and explain some of God's moral attributes.

5. Explain this statement: "God is one being, but He exists in three persons."

6. How do the members of the Trinity relate to each other?

7. What is the difference between God's directive will and His permissive will? What biblical passages support your explanation?

8. "God's foreknowledge is not in itself the cause of what happens." How does this statement help you understand free will?

9. How does your understanding of God's natural and moral attributes influence your daily life?

10. How does your understanding of the Trinity and God's will influence your daily life? Specifically meditate on each: Father, Son, Holy Spirit

---

There is a "God-shaped vacuum" in everyone that only He can fill.

Chapter 3

Theme: Everything about Christianity is determined by the person and work of Jesus Christ.

1. List and explain four ways in which Jesus proved He is fully God.

2. How do we know that Jesus was also fully human?

3. Why does it matter that Jesus was fully human?

4. Explain one of the heresies regarding God's nature. What could you say to someone who adhered to such a view?

5. What are three reasons Jesus had to live a perfect life?

6. How can you know that the Resurrection is *fact*, not fiction?

7. What difference does the Resurrection make to you?

8. Now that Jesus has ascended to heaven, what roles does He assume?

9. How often do you take advantage of your "free and confident access into the very presence of God?" Do you need to make some changes? How will you do it?

10. Assume that you have a non-Christian friend who asks you, "Who is Jesus? Why should I believe in Him?" How would you respond, based on the information in this chapter?

It doesn't matter what you think of Play-Doh®, Napoleon, or Richard Nixon. It does matter what you think of Jesus Christ.

Chapter 4

Theme: The cross of Christ has been called the central fact of Christianity.

1. When the cross of Jesus Christ is called "the central fact of human history," what does that mean?

2. Why is Christ's death also the central fact of Christianity?

3. How did Christ's death fulfill the Old Testament sacrificial system?

4. How do the terms listed below describe Christ's death on the cross?

atonement	ransom
reconciliation	substitution
appeasement	

5. Explain one of the theories that people have used throughout history to minimize the importance of Christ's death on the cross.

6. How would you answer a friend who asked you, "Why was the cross necessary? Why couldn't God just forgive?"

7. How would you answer a friend who asked you, "How could one person die to save the whole world?"

8. "The Gospel is not Christ 'plus' something, as good as that something may be." What does that statement mean?

9. What does Christ's death mean to you?

10. Think of someone you know who needs to hear about Jesus Christ's death on the cross. Pray for that person. How might you tell your own experience of Jesus Christ?

> *The Gospel is not a set of swimming instructions to a drowning person. It is the God-man jumping in and rescuing a drowning person.*

Chapter 5

Theme: Each of us is a personality created by God in His own image. We have the ability to sin, and we have the ability to accept God's grace.

1. How are those around you trying to answer the question, "Who am I?"

2. How did God create man as unique from the rest of creation?

3. Explain this statement: "The image of God in man has to do, rather, with personality."

4. In addition to being created like God in personality, how else were we created in God's image?

5. Explain the statement: "The sin of Adam and Eve . . . was something for which they were personally responsible."

6. Describe some of the results of man's fall, his disobeying God.

7. How would you define the term *total depravity?*

8. Summarize in a sentence or two Augustine's view of the Fall.

9. If Adam's legacy was sin, what was Jesus' legacy?

10. What would be your description of the grandeur of God's grace? Have you experienced this in your own life? If not, what is keeping you from doing so? If you have, describe what happened.

> *For every look you take at your own tendency to sin, take ten looks at the magnificent sacrifice of Christ for you.*

Chapter 6

Theme: Understanding who the Holy Spirit is and what He does will strengthen our relationship with Him, bringing us power, joy, and hope.

1. Why is it important to know that the Holy Spirit is a personality?

2. How is the Holy Spirit also Deity?

3. List and explain the five aspects of the Holy Spirit's work in the Old Testament.

4. Explain the statement: "In the Old Testament the Holy Spirit came on individuals temporarily."

5. Describe the New Testament arrival of the Holy Spirit. How does this compare to the arrival of the Holy Spirit in the Old Testament?

6. List and describe three ways the Holy Spirit convicts us. Describe a specific time when the Holy Spirit convicted you.

7. Read 1 Corinthians 14. Which of these gifts has the Holy Spirit given you? From Galatians 5:22-23, give examples of which *fruit* of the Spirit you would like to develop.

8. Explain this statement: "By misunderstanding the role of the Holy Spirit in interpreting the Scriptures, some have made the Bible almost a magical book, equating their subjective feelings with the authority of the Spirit."

9. When are we sealed, indwelt, and baptized by the Holy Spirit?

10. "The test as to whether or not you are filled with the Spirit is not, 'Have you received an external sign or been given a particular gift of the Spirit?' The test is rather, 'Have you given yourself wholly and without reservation to God?'" Do you pass the test of being filled with the Holy Spirit? If you do not, what can you begin to do differently today?

The most difficult thing in the world is to try to live the Christian life without the power of the Holy Spirit.

Chapter 7

Theme: Salvation is a truth that must be understood with the mind and with the heart. It has a permanent, profound impact on those who experience it.

1. Think back to your own salvation experience. What drew you to God? Did you fully understand your salvation? If you did not fully understand it, when did it become more clear to you?

2. Explain the meaning of the word *repentance* in practical terms.

3. How did your intellect, your emotions, and your will play a part in your repentance?

4. Explain this sentence: "Faith is central to the whole Christian experience."

5. What are the elements of saving faith? What are the results of saving faith?

6. How would you describe a born-again person? (See 2 Peter 1:4; 2 Cor. 5:17; Eph. 4:2; Col. 3:10.)

7. Explain the terms *election*, *predestination*, and *foreknowledge* as they relate to salvation.

8. Explain the terms *justification*, *sanctification*, and *glorification* as they relate to salvation.

9. How is God sanctifying you? How are you reacting to His work in your life?

10. Think of one person you know who has not experienced God's salvation. Write down some key truths you would like to share with this person from your own experience. Then begin to pray for the opportunity to speak about the great gift of salvation.

The greatest favor you can do for someone is to introduce him or her to Jesus Christ.

Chapter 8

Theme: Often misrepresented in the media, angels are objective realities, used by God as messengers and servants. Satan is also an objective reality.

1. What does the media say about angels? Think about specific examples.

2. How does the author of this book compare an angel to an express mail driver?

3. Describe five attributes of angels. Now describe specific instances when the media strayed from these biblical characteristics.

4. Describe the three facets of angelic activity.

5. What does the Bible tell us about the two angels Michael and Gabriel?

6. List and describe two common misconceptions about angels.

7. What are some of the names used for Satan, a fallen angel? What do these names mean?

8. List and explain four biblical truths about Satan.

9. How would you explain the following sentence: "We can avoid the extreme of trying to see Satan behind every misfortune without recognizing our personal responsibility and choice for our actions"?

10. As you struggle to run the Christian race, in what ways do you defend yourself against Satan? Do you need to renew your mind (Rom. 12:2)? Are there tempting circumstances you need to avoid? What ways can you remind yourself of Jesus' victory?

> *Angels take pleasure in God's gift of salvation to us and even rejoice when one sinner repents!*

Chapter 9

Theme: The church is people who have been called out to Jesus Christ; it is not a building.

1. How does the word *ekklesia* describe the church?

2. Describe and compare the church in the Old Testament with the church in the New Testament.

3. Where and when was the first church born?

4. Explain how the following verses describe the first church: "I now realize how true it is that God does not show favoritism but accepts men from every nation who fear him and do what is right" (Acts 10:34-35).

5. How do the following metaphors describe the church?
- The body of Christ (1 Cor. 12:12-31)
- The building of God (1 Peter 2:5; 1 Cor. 6:19-20)
- The bride of Christ (Eph. 5:25-27, 31-32; 2 Cor. 11:2; Rev. 19:7, 22:17)

6. Describe the activities of the first church.

7. Describe the five membership requirements of the first church. How do these requirements compare to the membership requirements of the church today?

8. Explain the following three systems of church government:
- Episcopalianism
- Presbyterianism
- Congregationalism

9. What do you think of this statement: "There is no such thing as a lone-wolf Christian."

10. Examine your own view of church. Do you see church more as a building or as people gathered together? Why are you part of the church? What are you gaining spiritually and how are you serving in your church? Do you need to make some changes?

Hot coals increase in heat as they are clumped together; alone they grow cold.

Chapter 10

Theme: When Jesus comes again, believers will be judged and then enjoy eternity with God in heaven. Unbelievers will also be judged and then spend eternity in hell.

1. Explain this sentence: "Both Old and New Testaments contend that history is moving to a climax and the sovereign God is in control."

2. How is the fact that Christ is coming again an incentive for holy living? In what ways has this fact affected your daily life?

3. How would you explain the following terms: *the Tribulation* and *the Rapture?*

4. Define and explain the following terms: *pretribulation, midtribulation,* and *posttribulation.*

5. What is the difference between premillennialism, amillennialism, and postmillennialism?

6. What happens to believers' bodies when they are resurrected?

7. What happens to dead believers before they are resurrected? What happens to dead unbelievers before they are resurrected?

8. How would you explain this sad fact: "There is no biblical evidence for believing in the final restoration of the lost or in the universal salvation of all men"? How can this reality encourage you to witness to unbelievers?

9. Describe heaven and what will happen to believers there. Also describe hell and what will happen to unbelievers there.

10. If Jesus came back today, do you know for certain that you would be with Him in heaven? If you are not certain, what would you need to do to become certain? Do you have a friend or family member who needs to hear about God's gift of salvation and promise of eternity in heaven? Ask the Lord to help you share the Good News with this person.

> *Heaven will be the perfection for which we have always longed.*